ay during the antebellum years, Lander
ays, many precedents in organization, mar-
eting, and personnel relations were estab-
shed which prevailed in the industry during
he great cotton mill boom near the end of
he nineteenth century.

Brief resumes of the history of each indi-
idual company within the state are included,
nd in many cases the author has supplied
eretofore missing information and has cor-
ected errors in traditional accounts.

Based on extensive research in early South
Carolina newspapers, numerous public and
private manuscript collections, and other
ources, *The Textile Industry in Antebellum
South Carolina* will be invaluable for all
cholars and laymen interested in the econo-
ny of the Old South.

ERNEST M. LANDER, JR., is professor of history at Clemson University. A native of Calhoun Falls, South Carolina, he received his
A.B. degree at Wofford College and his M.A.
and Ph.D. degrees at the University of North
Carolina. He has published extensively in historical quarterlies and other journals. He is
the author of *A History of South Carolina,
1865–1960* and is co-editor with C. M. Mc-
Gee, Jr., of *A Rebel Came Home: The Diary
of Floride Clemson.*

The Textile Industry
in Antebellum South Carolina

The Textile Industry in Antebellum South Carolina

ERNEST McPHERSON LANDER, JR.

BATON ROUGE
LOUISIANA STATE UNIVERSITY PRESS

Library of Congress Card Number: 69–12590
SBN 8071–0311–X
Manufactured in the United States of America by
Thos. J. Moran's Sons, Inc., Baton Rouge, La.

Designed by Barney McKee

Preface

It is well known that manufacturing made limited head-way in the antebellum South when compared with its progress in the North. Nevertheless, there were always Southerners who believed the prosperity of their region could be improved through increased industry and diversification of agriculture. From time to time war, low cotton prices, economic dependence on the North, or other factors prodded the Old South into brief flurries of industrial activity. These efforts were sometimes accompanied with much fanfare in Southern newspapers and journals.

Judged by the propaganda outpourings, the industry that seemed to attract the Southerners' greatest attention was cotton manufacturing. Prior to Whitney's gin a few entrepreneurs had attempted with primitive machinery to process the white staple into cloth. Thereafter, the lure beckoned periodically until the great cotton mill crusade of the 1880's assured the South of lasting success. Within South Carolina, textiles, despite much trial and error, secured a permanent foothold before 1860 and set many precedents followed by the larger entrepreneurs of the post-Civil War era.

In recent years several writers have published a limited number of articles and monographs on early textile development in the South, but no one has attempted to supersede Broadus Mitchell's pioneer study *The Rise of the Cotton Mills in the South*, published in 1921. In fact, no one has produced a comprehensive study of antebellum textiles in a single Southern state. As the textile development in South Carolina was fairly typical of other Southeastern states, I hope my monograph will prove useful for considering the region as a whole. There is one significant difference: No other Southern state produced a textile entrepreneur with the energy and vision of William Gregg.

In dealing with textiles in antebellum South Carolina, I have made extensive use of important source materials generally by-passed by other writers: manuscript census returns for 1840, 1850, and 1860 (more accurate and complete than published returns) and county courthouse records (deeds and wills). Additionally, I have searched early South Carolina newspapers, including the valuable Charleston *Courier*, a strong supporter of industry, and I have investigated numerous public and private manuscript collections. My study includes summaries, generalizations, and some comparisons with other states. I have also attempted to give brief resumés of the history of each individual company within South Carolina, at times supplying missing information and correcting errors in traditional accounts. I have not cited the *Statutes at Large of South Carolina* (12 vols.; Columbia, S.C., 1836–41, 1873–74) for charters of incorporation, as the *Statutes* are well indexed.

Much of the research herein was undertaken two decades ago as part of my Ph.D. dissertation ("Manufacturing in Antebellum South Carolina") at the University of North Carolina. Although I published a few brief articles on early textiles in South Carolina, I became convinced that I needed to make further study before attempting to tell the full story. I laid the work aside and only recently did I return to it to finish the research.

For this publication I am indebted to many persons for aid and advice. Chancellor J. Carlyle Sitterson and the late Dr. Albert Ray Newsome, of the University of North Carolina, Chapel Hill, patiently guided my work on the doctoral dissertation. Dr. Gustavus G. Williamson, Jr., Virginia Polytechnic Institute, read the finished manuscript and offered valuable suggestions as to content and organization, many of which I have incorporated herein. William C. Lott graciously made the Graniteville Company's archives available to me. Graniteville has the most important collection of antebellum industrial records extant in South Carolina.

Others who aided me in various ways include Julian Hennig, Columbia; Wayne Freeman of the Greenville *News*; T. R. Waring of the Charleston *News and Courier;* Hubert Hendrix of the Spartanburg *Herald;* Franklin Acker of the Anderson *Independent;* Mrs. Marshall P. Orr, Anderson; Mrs. Frank Farmer, Anderson; Miss Sarah Nash, Fountain Inn; Mrs. Roy Lister, Greer; Miss Mary Riley, Anderson; David Reid, Converse College, Spartanburg; the R. L. Bryan Company, Columbia; John S. Taylor, Greenville; Miss Hazel Jones, Greenville; William D. Anderson, Gastonia, N. C.; and the following deceased persons; Dr. D. D. Wallace, Wofford College, Spartanburg; T. E. Keitt, Newberry; H. B. Carlisle, Spartanburg; Mrs. Helen K. Hennig, Columbia; Mrs. T. J. Mauldin, Pickens; and E. N. Sitton, Anderson.

Mrs. Ruby Lott and Mrs. Beth Stanzione typed the manuscript, and my wife Sarah spent endless hours combing old newspaper files and proofreading. Finally, I am indebted to the Clemson University Alumni Loyalty Fund, whose financial support helped defray the expense of publication.

E.M.L., Jr.

Contents

The Textile Industry
in Antebellum South Carolina

Chapter 1 From Cottage to Factory

For several decades after the original colonization of South Carolina, the colonists depended largely on England for textiles. Undoubtedly, however, there was some home spinning and weaving in the outlying districts at an early date, and as the colony expanded, so did its domestic industry. Shortly before the end of the colonial era, Governor William Bull reported that looms were to be seen in "almost every house in our Western settlement." [1] There was also some textile manufacturing in the low country because the French and Indian War and high insurance rates had greatly increased the cost of imported goods. A few planters organized teams of slaves to spin and weave under one roof. For example, Daniel Heyward in 1776 placed thirty Negroes under the supervision of a white woman spinner and a white male weaver. He hoped to be able to supply his neighbors, but the Revolution interrupted his enterprise. On February 19, 1777, he wrote: "My manufactory goes on bravely, but fear the want of cards will put a stop to it, as they are not to be got; if they were there is not the least doubt that we could make six thousand yards of good cloth in the year from the time we began." [2]

Fragmentary evidence indicates that Pierre Guiraud owned a "stocking-weiving" (knitting?) factory in Charleston during the Revolution, that a Mrs. Ramage manufactured cloth on James Island in 1789, and that some Irishmen operated a weaving

---

[1] William Bull to Commissioners of Trade and Plantations, September 6, 1768 (Photostatic copy in Public Colonial Records of South Carolina, South Carolina Department of Archives and History, Columbia), XXXII, 30–32.

[2] David D. Wallace, *The History of South Carolina* (4 vols.; New York, 1934), II, 407; August Kohn, *The Cotton Mills of South Carolina* (Columbia, S.C., 1907), 7. Kohn's monograph contains valuable information about the early South Carolina textile industry. It is based on manuscript materials, some of which are no longer available.

shop in Williamsburg District. Guiraud's shop was destroyed in the British siege of Charleston. Nothing else is known of these early ventures, not even the type of yarn used.[3]

One projected enterprise, novel for South Carolina, was Lewis Newhouse's proposal to set up a "cotton and linnen printing manufactory." In 1785 he unsuccesfully petitioned the General Assembly for financial aid, including 20,000 acres of land on which to grow provisions for his skilled workers, who were to be imported from Switzerland. In another case William Mc-Clure migrated from Rhode Island to Laurens District for the purpose of establishing a cotton and woolen mill. Unfortunately, he claimed the cost of the machinery as well as the transportation costs for his family had rendered him "utterly unable to Complete the necessary machines or carry on the Business so that it may be of public Utility." The legislature thereupon authorized him to raise £400 via a lottery with the provision that he train seven white apprentices for seven years.[4] There is no evidence that either Newhouse or McClure ever began operations.

None of these early textile ventures could be called factories in the modern sense of the word, for none used power-driven machinery. This situation began to change shortly after the Revolution with the introduction of the spinning jenny, which had been invented in England in 1767. One of the earliest American factories to use the jenny was established at Stateburg in Sumter District. A correspondent for the *American Museum* wrote in 1790 that a "gentleman of great mechanical knowledge"

[3] Wallace, *History of South Carolina*, II, 407–408. Guiraud unsuccessfully sought financial aid from the General Assembly to re-establish himself. Petition of Pierre Guiraud to General Assembly, January 22, 1789 (MS in "Public Improvements: Manufacturing" File, South Carolina Department of Archives and History).

[4] Petitions of Lewis Newhouse and William McClure to General Assembly, January 22, 1785, and December 2, 1794 (MSS in "Public Improvements: Manufacturing" File); Journals of the Senate, 1795 (MS in South Carolina Department of Archives and History), 180.

and instructed in most of the branches of cotton manufacturing in Europe had completed and put into operation ginning, carding, slugging, and two spinning machines of 84 spindles each. Water power propelled the machinery.[5] The "gentleman" referred to was undoubtedly Hugh Templeton, one of the partners of the company. The previous year he had asked the legislature for an exclusive patent to build and sell cotton carding and cotton spinning machines in South Carolina. He claimed to have constructed both types and to have introduced them into the state. Other leading investors in his enterprise were John Mac-Nair and Benjamin Waring, an entrepreneur and planter of prominence.[6]

Within two years of its organization the partnership was dissolved, leaving Templeton and MacNair sole owners of the factory. They moved the machinery to MacNair's plantation a short distance away, and there they resumed operations. But the two proprietors immediately encountered new difficulties because of an unstable and costly labor supply. According to their account, they employed and trained several slaves to run the equipment, only to have the slave-owners withdraw the blacks; thus the process of employing and training had to be repeated. In dire need they appealed to the General Assembly for aid. A sympathetic committee in the House recommended a loan of £1,200, but the Senate refused financial assistance as inconsistent "with the justice due to the Creditors of the State." Nonetheless, the two partners struggled on until MacNair's death in 1795. MacNair's widow and son-in-law then bought the machinery for approximately £15. This low price indicates that the machinery was fairly simple and that the enterprise had

[5] *American Museum,* VIII (July–December, 1790), Appendix IV, 12.
[6] Petition of Hugh Templeton to General Assembly, 1789 (MS in "Public Improvements: Inventions" File, South Carolina Department of Archives and History). The Senate failed to grant Templeton's monopoly. See Journals of the Senate, 1789 (MS in South Carolina Department of Archives and History), 200. The Stateburg story was later told by John B. Miller, MacNair's stepson. See Charleston *Courier,* February 26, 1845.

proved to be unprofitable. Eventually the machinery was shipped to Lincolnton, North Carolina.[7] In his book *A View of South-Carolina, as Respects Her Natural and Civil Concerns,* John Drayton declared that the factory "bid fair to rise into consideration" but "the price of labour was too great, to permit its goods to stand any competition with those of similar qualities, which were imported from Great Britain and this, with a want of public patronage, led to its being discontinued." [8]

Unfortunately, information available today about the Stateburg entrepreneurs is fragmentary. Who was Hugh Templeton? In retrospect he gives the appearance of having been a mechanical genius. Where did he learn his trade? These and other questions cannot be answered. One final comment may be made that this small venture was attempted at the same time Samuel Slater and Moses Brown launched their first Rhode Island textile mill. But, whereas Slater and Brown were successful and ushered in an era of textile growth in New England, the Stateburg mill failed. For some years after, so far as records reveal, no other South Carolinians attempted to establish a textile factory. The advent of Whitney's gin diverted their attention to the more lucrative business of growing cotton.

The Napoleonic Wars, accompanied by President Jefferson's Embargo Act of 1807, sped up New England textile production and again turned some South Carolina entrepreneurs toward cotton manufacturing. In 1808 an ambitious textile undertaking was attempted in Charleston under the name of the South Carolina

[7] Petition of Templeton and MacNair to General Assembly, December, 1792, and House Committee Report, December 13, 1792 (MSS in "Public Improvements: Manufacturing" File); Journals of the Senate, 1792 (MS in South Carolina Department of Archives and History), 113–14, 135; Charleston *Courier,* February 26, 1845. An inventory of MacNair's goods sold July 30, 1795, and February 25, 1797, includes the machinery (MSS in John MacNair Papers, Duke University Library).

[8] John Drayton, *A View of South-Carolina, as Respects Her Natural and Civil Concerns.* (Charleston, S.C., 1802), 149. In a survey of the state Drayton noted no other cotton mills. He found and listed five fulling mills in the upcountry. See pp. 152–53.

Homespun Company.[9] It came into being as a direct result of the Embargo, favorable publicity by the Charleston *City Gazette*, and the hard organizational work done by Dr. John L. E. W. Shecut, a scientist and man of letters, who in his enthusiasm for the project named one of his daughters "Carolina Homespun." A number of other Charleston civic leaders[10] were also involved in the company.

At a public meeting on August 1, 1808, the promoters recommended capitalization of $150,000 in shares of $10 each, payable in five installments. Despite much fanfare the stock sold slowly. Only $21,730 was pledged and of that amount only $4,356 was collected by mid-September. Shecut, in a series of public letters, emphasized potential profits rather than patriotism. He also furnished information purporting to show that a 1,000-spindle, 40-loom, tidewater-power mill could be constructed for $28,000, and thus persuaded the stockholders, despite limited resources, to go ahead with construction. In addition, the stockholders elected Shecut to replace Dr. David Ramsay as president.

On October 24 of that year the promoters laid the cornerstone of their brick factory amid great ceremony and listened to an address by William Loughton Smith, prominent South Carolina Federalist leader and former United States Congressman. In

[9] There is evidence that a Dr. Le Seigneur attempted to manufacture cotton in Charleston in 1807, but apparently his machinery was lost in passage from Europe. Colonel Thomas Taylor was reputed to have started a small mill at Columbia about this time. See John L. E. W. Shecut, *Medical and Philosophical Essays* (Charleston, S.C., 1819), 12; F. DeVere Smith, "Columbia, South Carolina: Early Textile Center," *Textile History Review,* IV (July, 1963), 109.

[10] A detailed account based primarily on newspaper sources is Richard W. Griffin, "An Origin of the New South: The South Carolina Homespun Company, 1808–1815," *Business History Review,* XXXV (Autumn, 1961), 402–14. Shecut's own account appeared in the Charleston *City Gazette,* August 18, 21, 25, September 5, 8, 1810, and was reprinted in *Textile History Review,* III (July, 1962), 162–70. Other prominent stockholders included John Horlbeck, Jr., Jonathan Lucas, Jr., Thomas Bennett, Jr., Simon Magwood, Joseph Kirkland, George Warren Cross, and Dr. David Ramsay.

lauding the efforts of the Charleston businessmen, Smith foresaw a new era of commercial independence, reminiscent of Alexander Hamilton's dream in the 1790's. He said, "We have long known that we possess, in the bosom of our soil, inexhaustible resources; we now know, and feel, that we have, in our own bosoms, a spirit of patriotism to call forth these resources, and to make them instrumental to the security of our rights and to the avenging of our wrongs. The shuttle and the loom, operating on the products of your fields and your flocks, will in this century, emancipate you from commercial thraldom, as the operations of your arsenals and foundries delivered you, in the last, from political slavery." [11]

The promoters next requested the legislature for an act of incorporation, averring a desire to place the country beyond the "paralyzing touch or control of any Foreign power." They also invited the state to subscribe to their stock. The General Assembly granted a twenty-one-year charter but refused to invest.[12]

Almost immediately, problems began to plague the inexperienced entrepreneurs. As Shecut later explained, the company collected only $27,000; the land and buildings cost $12,000— a severe drain on their capital; attempts to manufacture machinery locally proved a time-consuming failure; and eventually the company spent $6,000 for machinery imported from the North. The directors, determined to give the factory a fair trial, installed the equipment, including 250 spindles, and began operations. They encountered difficulties, about which Shecut did not elaborate, with their Yankee laborers. But even more disastrous to their fortunes was the lack of a proper propelling power. The directors had planned to use tidewater power from a large marsh pond. The city council had granted them a thirty-

[11] For Smith's address see George C. Rogers, Jr., *Evolution of a Federalist: William Loughton Smith of Charleston (1758–1812)* (Columbia, S.C., 1962), 378–79, quoting Charleston *Courier*, October 31, 1808.
[12] Petition of South Carolina Homespun Company to General Assembly, 1808, (MS in "Public Improvements: Manufacturing" File).

year lease on the marsh, only too late to find that the property was claimed by other persons. The directors were thus forced to fall back on mule power, which proved to be an unsatisfactory arrangement. Here was an early instance, to be repeated numerous times, wherein a Southern tidewater mill was at a disadvantage in competing with New England mills because of inadequate power. The Northerners were able to use the ample water power to be found near the coast. Another error of the Homespun directors was the use of costly long-staple cotton in the production of osnaburgs. By and large, they found that the cost to manufacture osnaburgs was 37½ cents per yard, or 7½ cents above the usual market price.

In 1809 the company, under its new president, John Johnson, Jr., launched another appeal for state aid—a loan of $5,000.[13] Again the General Assembly refused to be drawn into the ill-fated scheme. Two years of operations ate up the company's remaining capital of $9,000, forcing the stockholders in 1810 to face bankruptcy or reorganization. In August the ever-optimistic Shecut offered the owners a new plan whereby the hiring of additional mules and Negro boys, the elimination of expensive long-staple cotton from production, and the purchase of a carding machine would, he maintained, effect sufficient savings to yield a satisfactory profit. He pleaded for an additional $6,000 investment, pointing out that a sale of the company's real estate would probably bring no more than $6,000—hardly enough to begin operations anew in a rented building on a less expensive site, as some stockholders were suggesting.

Dissension and disappointment among the stockholders doomed the attempt to secure additional capital. The company, once more under Shecut's presidency, made another appeal to the legislature, which, this time, authorized a lottery but provided nothing further.[14] As this scheme did not materialize, the

[13] Petition of John Johnson, Jr., to the Senate, 1809 (MS in "Public Improvements: Manufacturing" File).
[14] Petition of John L. E. W. Shecut and others to General Assembly, November 28, 1810, ibid.

stockholders suspended operations within a year or two and decided to sell out. They eventually recovered but little of their capital.[15]

The War of 1812, as the Embargo had done previously, created new interest in textile manufacturing in South Carolina. Several small factories were consequently built during the conflict. Best known of these was Governor David R. Williams' mill on Cedar Creek near Society Hill. Williams formed a partnership with William Matthews, a small-time textile operator, and constructed a factory building during the summer of 1814. According to traditional accounts, Williams' carpenters erected the five-story building with lumber from his sawmill. The war blockade delayed the arrival of the Northern-made machinery, which had to be hauled by slow freight overland. When all was ready, a Northern superintendent came down and trained Negro operatives, one of whom reputedly became superintendent himself sometime later. A news account in early 1816 stated that the factory had three to four hundred spindles in operation.[16]

Williams and Matthews marketed some of their goods at the factory; some they sent by boat down-river, and some went inland by wagon. Their most ambitious sales adventure was to seek a Navy contract for sail cloth. Matthews sent several hundred yards of cloth to the naval commander in Charleston, who was impressed. Secretary of the Navy William Jones also showed interest, but no contract was forthcoming. The prospects were probably ruined by the coming of peace. The partners did not continue to operate the factory for long after normal trade with Europe resumed. This turn in economic fortune made it more profitable for Williams to employ his slaves in cotton growing than in cotton manufacturing.[17]

[15] The company purchased the land for $4,825 in September, 1808, and sold it, with buildings, for $8,000 in December, 1815. Charleston Deeds, Y-7, 189–90, M-8, 394–95.

[16] Harvey T. Cook, *The Life and Legacy of David Rogerson Williams* (New York, 1916), 140; Columbia *Telescope*, March 5, 1816.

[17] Cook, *David Rogerson Williams*, 141; Robert Mills, *Statistics of South Carolina, Including a View of Its Natural, Civil, and Military History,*

William Mayrant's factory in Sumter District followed a similar pattern. Begun in 1814 under the name of the Sumter Manufacturing Company, the enterprise had at least seven other partners, but Mayrant shortly became sole proprietor of the venture. He encountered the usual difficulties, expense, and delay in procuring suitable machinery and in actually getting started. Moreover, his difficulties were compounded when he tried to manage the business while serving a term in Congress. As did Williams and Matthews, he hired experienced Yankee workers to come South with the machinery and train Negro operatives. Tradition credits his failure to the use of horses rather than water power, but it is more likely he simply could not compete favorably after 1815 with cheaper-made English goods. In these post-war years many New England mills also failed. In 1821 Mayrant sold the machinery for $8,000 to the Reverend Thomas Hutchings and John M. Courcier, who immediately moved it to Greenville District. The inventory furnished included 720 spindles, several drawing and roving frames, cards, reels, and a stretcher, thus making it the best equipped cotton mill in South Carolina to that date.[18]

In the meantime Peter Gibert built a cotton mill on Little River in Abbeville District. Robert Mills, in writing his *Statistics of South Carolina*, reported that Gibert "had the whole work, castings, turnings, etc. executed on the spot; an instance of con siderable ingenuity and enterprise." This mill also ceased to operate after the War of 1812. [19] In nearby Greenville District, Adam Carruth, a gun manufacturer; Waddy Thompson, a fu-

---

General and Particular (Charleston, S.C., 1826), 515-16; David R. Williams to William Jones, August 13, 1814, and undated reply (Photostatic copy in possession of Julian Hennig, Columbia, S.C.).

[18] Richard W. Griffin, "Research in Industrial History: The American Textile Industry, 1820-1833," *Textile History Review*, IV (April, 1963), 85-99; Ernest M. Lander, Jr., ed., "Two Letters by William Mayrant on His Cotton Factory, 1815," *South Carolina Historical Magazine*, LIV (January, 1953), 1-5.

[19] Mills, *Statistics of South Carolina*, 353-54; Abbeville Wills, Box 39, Pkg. 830.

ture Congressman; and others petitioned the legislature for aid in setting up a textile factory. In December, 1812, the General Assembly appropriated $10,000 to be paid to the petitioners for the purpose of establishing a mill of not less than five hundred spindles. For reasons unknown today, Carruth, Thompson, and their associates failed to carry out their plans.[20]

In sum, the early textile mills of South Carolina were small affairs which at best enjoyed only a temporary success. They obtained most of their machinery and skilled labor from the North, and several sought, with meager results, state financial aid. They operated with insufficient capital and often with inadequate power. They experimented with slave labor, and, so far as can be told, experienced poor management. Above all, they were especially hard hit by keen English competition in peacetime. In view of the failure of the South Carolina Homespun Company, Dr. John Shecut bitterly concluded: "This experiment, although attempted under the most favorable auspicies, proved to a demonstration that South-Carolina was not prepared to become a manufacturing state." [21] But even as he wrote those lines, several small textile plants were getting into operation in the back country.

[20] Petition of Adam Carruth and others to General Assembly, 1812 (MS in "Public Improvements: Manufacturing" File).
[21] Shecut, Medical and Philosophical Essays, 26.

Chapter 2 Piedmont Pioneers

Renewed English competition in 1815, which quickly forced the closing of Governor Williams' and Congressman Mayrant's small factories, similarly affected the textile operations in New England. The depression in that area lasted until 1821 and ruined many marginal producers. As a result, a number of Yankee entrepreneurs moved South in search of more advantageous locations for manufacturing.[1] Several such adventurers entered South Carolina and established small cotton mills in the Piedmont region of the state. In most instances they were aided by local capital, management, and labor. Records reveal that eighteen separate cotton mills were put into operation between 1816 and 1839 in the adjoining districts of Laurens, Spartanburg, Greenville, and Pendleton. Depression, fire, insufficient capital, and poor management wrecked some of these ventures, and the movement slowed perceptibly after 1839. Nevertheless, the cotton textile industry gained a small but permanent foothold in the Piedmont during the years 1816–40.

The first group to arrive in South Carolina included three brothers, Philip, Lindsey, and Wilbur Weaver, Thomas Slack, Leonard Hill, the Rev. Thomas Hutchings, and others, all apparently from Rhode Island.[2] Bringing machinery with them, they moved into Spartanburg District, drove down stakes on the banks of the Tyger River six miles above Cross Keys Post Office, and immediately began operations. In November, 1816, they announced that the South Carolina Cotton Manufactory, complete with five hundred spindles, would be ready for business by De-

[1] Caroline F. Ware, *The Early New England Cotton Manufacture: A Study in Industrial Beginnings* (Boston and New York, 1931), 56–79.

[2] Between 1816 and 1821 at least thirteen more men, including William Bates and the Weavers' brother, John, were connected with the group. How many came with the original band cannot be determined. Philip Weaver's Account Book, 1813–21 (MS in Wofford College Library, Spartanburg, S.C.).

cember 20. Richard Pearce was designated as their Charleston agent, and Philip Weaver was to be their agent at the factory.[3] The latter, by self-appointment or otherwise, assumed leadership of this vanguard, which was thereafter commonly known as the "Weavers."

Misfortune dogged the enterprise from its beginning. The Weavers, dependent on local capital, soon lost control of the factory. In fact, the property changed hands several times. Its financial backers included William Y. Davis, Benjamin Wofford, a wealthy Methodist clergyman, and the Charleston firm of McDowell and Black. By 1820 Thomas Slack had secured control of the factory, and that same year he sold it with three hundred acres of land back to Philip and John Weaver for $15,000.[4]

The new arrangement, however, was short lived. Philip Weaver had tired of the South. Perhaps the change in Southern outlook following the Panic of 1819 and the debate over Missouri statehood affected his attitude. At any rate he wrote that he yearned for a home in a free state "where myself & family will not be looked down upon with contempt because I am opposed to the abominable Practice of slavery." Probably before the end of 1821 he left South Carolina. Meanwhile, his brother John moved into Greenville District and set up a small cotton mill.[5] Further information about the Weavers' Spartanburg enterprise is scarce, but contemporary records reveal that between 1816 and 1826 the Weavers operated two factories at different points on the Tyger, both of which were destroyed by fire.[6]

The second partnership to establish a cotton mill in Spartanburg District was composed of John Clark, William B. Sheldon,

[3] Charleston *Courier*, November 23, 1816.

[4] Spartanburg Deeds, Q, 320–21, R, 12; Mortgage Book PPP (MS in South Carolina Department of Archives and History), 430. John Weaver had just recently arrived from the North. See Philip Weaver's Account Book.

[5] Undated letter in Philip Weaver's Account Book.

[6] One of the two mills was operating as late as 1825. As of April 3, 1826, Nathaniel Gist became the owner of the land on which both mills stood. He had purchased one tract in 1818. Spartanburg Deeds, Q, 320–21, T, 372–73. Mills, *Statistics of South Carolina*, 730.

and George and Leonard Hill, all of whom were master mechanics and manufacturers from near Providence, Rhode Island. Leonard Hill, who had been one of the Weavers' original partners, was chosen foreman, or business manager. This new group also brought their machinery from Rhode Island. From Columbia they carted it to a place on the Tyger about four miles above the Weavers' establishment. There, in January, 1819, they bought 125 acres of land from Isaac Crow and set up the Industry Cotton Manufacturing Company, more frequently called Hill and Clark, or simply Hill's factory. So short were they of funds at that time that they were forced to mortgage the property to Crow.[7]

The partnership agreement soon proved unsatisfactory to all concerned. The factory was in operation hardly a year before Sheldon sold his interest to Clark and departed for nearby Laurens District to run a small wool carding shop. In 1825 George Hill returned North after he had disposed of his share to Leonard Hill and Clark. Finally, in 1830, Leonard Hill became the sole proprietor of the factory when Clark sold his part and left to join Sheldon in Laurens. The factory was a small affair, similar in size to the Weavers. In 1825 it contained 432 spindles and eight looms.[8]

In 1835 Leonard Hill decided to enlarge his operations. With James Edward Henry, James Nesbitt, and Simpson Bobo as his new partners, Hill petitioned the General Assembly to incorpo-

[7] Spartanburg Deeds, Q, 316–17, R, 79–84. The traditional account places the Hills' coming at the same time as the Weavers. It is based on the memory of William A. Hill, Leonard's grandson. See Dr. J. B. O. Landrum, *History of Spartanburg County; Embracing an Account of Many Important Events, and Biographical Sketches of Statesmen, Divines and Other Public Men, and the Names of Many Others Worthy of Record in the History of Their County* (Atlanta, 1900), 157–61. William A. Hill's story is slightly in error. There is no documentary evidence to indicate that the Hills began operations before 1819. Moreover, miscellaneous bills and receipts in the August Kohn Papers show them to have been purchasing equipment in Rhode Island in 1818. (MSS in possession of Julian Hennig, Columbia, S.C.).

[8] Spartanburg Deeds, T, 101–102, 282–84, U, 573–74; Laurens Deeds, L, 58, N, 128, O, 27; Landrum, *Spartanburg County*, 160.

rate the Spartanburg Cotton Manufacturing Company. Henry was a successful lawyer who had migrated from Rhode Island in 1816, and Bobo was an enterprising iron manufacturer. The legislature granted their request, but the company failed to begin operations, apparently due to a disagreement among the prospective stockholders. Undaunted, Hill sought to incorporate his own factory the following year, with authority to increase his capital to $100,000. Hill's friend Henry H. Thomson, a well-known legislator and sometime mayor of Spartanburg, pushed a satisfactory bill through the General Assembly, but, nevertheless, the new charter attracted no capital to the business. The veteran manufacturer remained sole owner of his factory until his death in 1840.[9]

The first cotton factory in adjoining Greenville District was possibly established by the Reverend Thomas Hutchings, a versatile character who had led a romantic and somewhat checkered career. After he had come South with the Weavers in 1816, his actions were more those of a back-country preacher than those of a successful manufacturer. As in the case of Leonard Hill, he soon broke away from the Weavers to try his fortunes elsewhere. Hutchings' first stop was on the nearby Enoree River just inside Greenville District where he purchased some three hundred acres of land from Charles Dean in February, 1820. Within two months he had a small factory in operation that consisted of 144 spindles and the complementary equipment. Hutchings' financial plight, however, forced him to mortgage the land to one creditor and the machinery to another.[10]

This establishment was too small for the visionary Hutchings, who seemed ever ready to promote some new enterprise. In the spring of 1821, with John M. Courcier as a partner, he purchased the machinery of Congressman William Mayrant's Sum-

[9] Petitions of Leonard Hill to General Assembly, 1835, 1836 (MSS in "Public Improvements: Manufacturing" File; *Speech of Maj. James Edward Henry, on Productive Corporations, Delivered at Spartanburgh Court House, February 1, 1841* (Greenville, S.C., 1841), 11–12; Laurens Deeds, N, 149.
[10] Greenville Deeds, L, 119–21, 153.

ter factory with its 720 spindles and moved it to the Enoree, where for a time the proprietors ran both mills. Hutchings redeemed the original mortgages on the small mill, but he was still unable to evade the seemingly irresistible clutches of a creditor. Mayrant, to secure payment of over $8,000 due him, took a mortgage on both mills in May, 1821. [11]

In June, 1821, Hutchings was in Pendleton District promoting a textile factory there. He and Levi Garrison purchased a mill site on the Little Beaverdam, a tributary of the Tugaloo River. How long Hutchings was a partner in the Garrison factory is not known, but his attachment was probably fleeting. A report on the mill in 1826 failed to mention his name, and when Garrison sold the land and machinery in 1833 Hutchings was not connected with the enterprise.[12]

Although fire reputedly destroyed the larger of Hutchings' two Enoree factories about 1825, he rebuilt on the same site and retained control for several years. Sometime before 1830 Josiah Kilgore and Philip C. Lester took over the title to his Enoree holdings. As the new owners were both men of property, they probably financed the rebuilding of the burned factory and, in the process, squeezed out Hutchings. For many years after, the mill was known as Lester's factory.[13]

After losing out to Lester and Kilgore, Hutchings, according to tradition, moved to a creek nearby and for a time operated another small mill.[14] Soon he was back in Spartanburg District, this time on a money-raising program to establish a Methodist church in Spartanburg. But the church did not deter him for any length of time, and the minister shortly turned again to textiles.

---

[11] *Ibid.*, 250–52.

[12] Anderson Deeds, P, 355, U, 270–72; Mills, *Statistics of South Carolina*, 677.

[13] Landrum, *Spartanburg County*, 161–62; Undated news clipping [ca. 1880] in H. P. Hammett Scrapbook (in possession of Mrs. M. P. Orr, Anderson, S. C.).

[14] It is not known what happened to Hutchings' smaller factory on the Enoree. Possibly he had retained title to it or its machinery, thus enabling his continued operations there.

He found new investors in Benjamin Wofford, Simpson Bobo, Elias C. Leitner, and H. J. Dean, and in 1838 they set up the South Tyger Cotton Manufactory at Cedar Hill. Strangely enough, however, the legislature refused to grant the partners a charter of incorporation.[15]

In 1840 Hutchings relinquished his interest in the factory at Cedar Hill to the original partners, who had been joined by James McMakin and Francis A. Weaver, son of the veteran manufacturer John Weaver. Unfortunately for Hutchings' career in the Methodist Episcopal pulpit, David W. Moore, a new investor at Cedar Hill, filed charges of fraud against the minister. Before a church conference in 1843 he accused Hutchings of selling the South Tyger Cotton Manufactory without fully listing its liabilities, whereupon a church committee investigated the charges and found Hutchings guilty. The conference then expelled him from the church.[16]

If Hutchings' cotton mill on the Enoree in early 1820 was truly the first in Greenville District, it barely preceded two other ventures. The first of these, a small plant at the site of present-day Fork Shoals on the Reedy River, was managed by Shubal F. Arnold. He probably began operations before June 12, 1820, for at that time he mortgaged the machinery to George Terry for payment of two notes totalling $258. On October 9 Arnold also mortgaged the same property to Hudson Berry, a prominent Greenville District landowner, investor, and magistrate. Arnold's plant consisted of one spinning frame of seventy-two

[15] Petition of Rev. Thomas Hutchings, and others, to General Assembly, September 4, 1838 (MS in "Public Improvements: Manufacturing" File); Landrum, *Spartanburg County*, 161–62; Fronde Kennedy, supervisor, *A History of Spartanburg County: Compiled by the Spartanburg Unit of the Writers' Program of the Work Projects Administration in the State of South Carolina* (Spartanburg, S.C., 1940), 59.

[16] Spartanburg Deeds, X, 323; David W. Moore to Methodist Quarterly Conference of Bethel Church, July 7, 1843 (undated news clipping in 1948 in possession of the now deceased H. B. Carlisle, Spartanburg, S.C.). After his expulsion, Hutchings moved to Georgia and preached from Protestant Methodist pulpits. *Carolina Spartan* (Spartanburg), May 20, 1869.

spindles, a roping frame, a drawing frame, and two cards. In time Berry and his sons came into exclusive possession of the mill and controlled it until 1852. Then, the father having died, the sons sold the factory for a mere $450, an indication that they had scarcely enlarged upon Arnold's operations three decades earlier.[17]

The other venture belonged to John Weaver, who, as noted earlier, left the original New England group on the Tyger and moved to Thompson's Beaverdam in Greenville District sometime in 1820 or 1821. In establishing his mill, Weaver secured financial assistance from Josiah Kilgore, who forced him into bankruptcy in 1830. At this juncture, William Bates, another

[17] Greenville Deeds, L, 162, 165; Greenville Wills, Apt. 8, File 541.

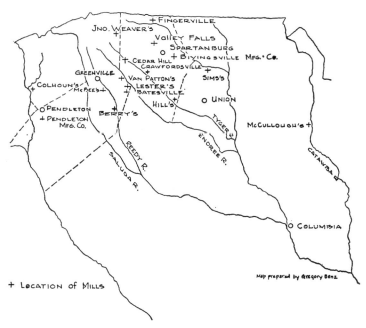

Map 1 The Piedmont or Back Country Textile Mills, 1840–1860.

former employee of the Weavers on the Tyger, stepped forward and at public sale purchased the entire establishment for only $1,235. Bates felt that the property was worth much more and, in a moment of altruism, decided to share the benefit of the purchase with the family of John Weaver, "by whose enterprise and industry the Said factory was established." He deeded a half interest in the mill and land to Weaver's son Francis. In return the father agreed to remain and assist in the management. Bates's generous move, however, proved unsatisfactory to both partners. Two years later, for $1,000, he sold his remaining interest in the land and building to Francis Weaver and departed. But with an eye toward future operations, Bates retained ownership of half of the machinery.[18] The elder Weaver remained on the place and operated the factory until the 1860's.

William Bates made a significant contribution to early Piedmont textile development, and his wanderings were wrought with as many tribulations as those of Hutchings. Coming from Rhode Island, where he had worked in cotton mills as an illiterate orphan since the age of eight, Bates landed in Charleston in 1819 with only two dollars in his possession. He was completely destitute by the time he reached the Weavers' factory on the Tyger. After he had labored there for two years, Bates moved upstream to work for Hill and Clark. By 1824 he had accumulated over five hundred dollars and joined Hugh Willson and William F. Downs to set up a small factory on Rabun's Creek in Laurens District.[19] This enterprise turned out to be a disastrous failure, and Bates lost all his hard-earned capital. Apparently inured to hardship, he started over again as a wage earner, this time in Dr. James Bivings' factory at Lincolnton, North Carolina. Presently, however, he returned to Spartanburg District and signed a three-year contract with Hill and Clark to oversee their Tyger River factory.[20]

[18] Greenville Deeds, R, 79–80, 100.
[19] Laurens Deeds, L, 152. Except wherein otherwise noted, information about Bates comes from Kennedy, *Spartanburg County*, 76–77.
[20] Contract dated September 17, 1827 (MS in August Kohn Papers).

As already noted, the tenacious Bates bought John Weaver's factory in 1830 and generously deeded a half interest to Weaver's son, only to find the arrangement unsuitable. He then moved to Lester's factory on the Enoree, but in 1833 he purchased three hundred acres of land from Josiah Kilgore on neighboring Rocky Creek.[21] There he built a cotton mill, moved his machinery from John Weaver's factory, and began operations. His new establishment immediately became known as Batesville. From time to time Bates expanded his factory, and when the Civil War erupted he was one of the most successful textile manufacturers in the state.

Probably the first cotton mill in the Piedmont to contain more than one thousand spindles was begun in 1836 by Dr. James Bivings, a public-spirited citizen of Lincolnton, North Carolina. As early as 1819 he had associated himself with Michael Schenck and John Hoke in the Lincoln Cotton Factory. In 1835 Dr. Bivings withdrew from the partnership, moved into Spartanburg District, secured local financial aid, and quietly purchased some 750 acres of land at the old site of Wofford's Iron Works on Lawson's Fork.[22]

In 1837 the General Assembly incorporated the Bivingsville Cotton Manufacturing Company, but under terms unacceptable to the stockholders. Hence, they sought and secured a revised charter in 1838 limiting their capital stock to $70,000 but not their liability. David Dantzler was elected as the corporation's first president. Other stockholders, besides Bivings, included James Edward Henry, H.J. Dean, Elias C. Leitner, and Simpson Bobo, several of whom were investors in textile mills elsewhere.[23] In fact, the opening of Bivingsville was probably one

21 Greenville Deeds, S, 23.
22 The price was $2,000. January 7, 1836, Spartanburg Deeds, W, 19. See also William L. Sherrill, *Annals of Lincoln County, North Carolina: Containing Interesting and Authentic Facts of Lincoln County History Through the Years 1749 to 1937* (Charlotte, N.C., 1937), 86, 495.
23 The first charter, incorporating the company at $100,000, restricted "corporate capacity" until all stock had been paid in. Moreover, it specified that Bivings, Bobo, and Leitner, the applicants, would have double liability.

reason why Leonard Hill had been unable to attract additional capital to his operations in 1836. Two of his prospective partners, Henry and Bobo, now teamed up with Dr. Bivings. When completed, the Bivingsville factory contained twelve hundred spindles and twenty-four looms, which had been purchased in Paterson, New Jersey. For power the plant depended on one, possibly two, overshot wheels which measured 26 feet in diameter and 12 feet wide. By 1840 the owners claimed to be processing six hundred bales of cotton annually.[24]

After Levi Garrison and Thomas Hutchings built a cotton factory in Pendleton District in 1821, no other mill was established in that district until 1829. At that time John Ewing Colhoun, a well-to-do planter and cousin of John C. Calhoun, formed a partnership with Thomas Elliot to operate a small woolen factory at Colhoun's mill seat five miles north of the village of Pendleton. Colhoun furnished the buildings and Negro operatives, while Elliot supplied the machinery and management. On May 6 Colhoun advertised that within a few days his factory would open "where Carding, Spinning, Weaving, Fulling, Dying and Dressing will be carried on by a Gentleman from the North well acquainted with the business." [25]

Colhoun quickly won acclaim for his products, especially his blankets which were made of part cotton and part wool. These won prizes at local fairs and also at an exhibition held at the Franklin Institute in Philadelphia. They were pronounced "by competent judges, to be equal, if not superior to London Duffils." [26] In spite of this happy beginning, Colhoun soon decided to give up manufacturing, averring that he had insufficient time to attend to his mill. In 1837 he advertised the machinery for

[24] Greenville *Mountaineer*, January 26, 1838, February 19, 1841; Landrum, *Spartanburg County*, 163.
[25] Pendleton *Messenger*, May 6, 1829.
[26] *Ibid.*, November 2, 1831; Charleston *Courier*, November 22, 1831; J. Leander Bishop, *A History of American Manufactures from 1608 to 1860*... (2 vols.; Philadelphia, 1861–64), II, 361.

sale but found no buyer. Three years later he leased the establishment to John Kershaw, whom he recommended to the public
as a man "skilful and capable of carrying on the business." [27]

While Colhoun was trying to sell his woolen machinery, a
group of citizens in Pendleton were promoting a larger factory
to be built south of the village. On land purchased in July, 1836,
Enoch B. Benson, and John T., Thomas M., and Benjamin F.
Sloan erected a two-story brick building and equipped it with
960 spindles which came from Paterson, New Jersey. Accompanying the machinery South were two experienced mechanics,
John Kershaw and William A. Bradley. After the installation of
the machinery Kershaw remained in Pendleton to train operatives but, as noted previously, in 1840 moved above Pendleton
to run Colhoun's woolen plant.[28]

Under the name of the Pendleton Manufacturing Company,
the partners, who now included William H. D. Gaillard, began
operations in January, 1838. The following December they
secured a charter of incorporation from the General Assembly,
authorizing a capital stock of $50,000 but with double liability
for each stockholder in event of failure.[29]

During the 1830's four more textile mills were set up in the
Piedmont—three in Greenville District and one in Laurens.
Vardry McBee built a small mill in 1832 on the Reedy River
just below the village of Greenville. McBee, who had spent
most of his life around Lincolnton, North Carolina, exhibited
good business foresight by investing $27,500 in Greenville real
estate in 1815. As the property increased in value, he invested in
other ventures, including railroads, flour mills, and paper manu-

[27]Pendleton *Messenger*, September 1, 1837, May 15, 1840. Sometime prior
to 1837 Colhoun replaced Elliot with one J. Rhodes, a former overseer or
worker at Vaucluse cotton factory near Augusta. Commonplace Book of
John E. Colhoun (MS in Clemson University Library), 62.
[28] A. J. Sitton, "A Partial History of the Pendleton Factory" (MS dated
December 25, 1888, in possession of the late E. N. Sitton, Anderson, S.C. in
1948).
[29] Pendleton *Messenger*, February 2, 1838.

facturing. By 1860 he was one of South Carolina's wealthiest citizens, although little of his wealth came from his modest cotton mill.[30]

The same year that McBee built his factory on the Reedy, Nicholas Van Patten, a native New Yorker, purchased land on the Enoree and set up quite an elaborate establishment which included a cotton mill, wool cards, a grist mill, a cotton gin, a machine shop, and a cabinet-maker's shop. He bridged the river and built several cabins, a storehouse, and a large residence. He boasted that the shoals where his plant was located was "one of the best water power sites" in the South. Nonetheless, when Van Patten offered the entire property for sale in 1838, he was able to dispose of only his textile machinery.[31]

Van Patten gave evidence of being a mechanical prodigy. For years he experimented with "a new principle in science which would revolutionize the machinery of the world" and made three trips to England in quest of further knowledge. He constructed model after model of his "perpetual motion" machine, constantly predicting he was on the verge of success, but ever failing. On the other hand, he claimed to have invented a number of attachments for cotton mills, only to be cheated out of them. Eccentric though he was, Van Patten was an ever-generous philanthropist and was highly respected in his community. He remained with his various enterprises on the Enoree until his death in 1889.[32]

In neighboring Laurens District, William F. Downs and R. F. Simpson erected a cotton mill in 1833, presumably on the same site where Downs and Bates had failed earlier. In 1836, after

[30] Sketch of McBee's life is in De Bow's Review, XIII (September, 1852), 314–18. In 1860 McBee's property was listed at $367,350. Eighth U. S. Census, Free Inhabitants, South Carolina: Greenville District (MS in National Archives).
[31] Laurens Deeds, M, 256; Greenville Mountaineer, September 21, 1838; Seventh Census, Products of Industry, South Carolina: Greenville District (MS in South Carolina Department of Archives and History).
[32] An account of Van Patten's philanthropies and business activities is in The Minutes of the Spartan Baptist Association of South Carolina 1963 (Spartanburg, S.C., 1963), 71–75.

William and Robert White had replaced Simpson as partners, fire completely destroyed the business. In a memorial to the legislature the partners claimed a loss of $17,000 to $18,000 by the fire after having enjoyed three prosperous years of milling. They requested permission to hold a lottery to obtain funds for re-establishing the mill. The legislature granted their request, but there is no evidence that they rebuilt the factory.[33]

The first back-country mills produced only coarse yarn, which was usually numbered 5 to 20, but as the industry became more firmly established, some mills also began to weave. The Hills had looms by 1825, and Colhoun installed looms from the beginning, as did Bivingsville. Prior to 1840, however, the majority continued to manufacture only yarn on equipment bought mainly in the North. The Hills and the Weavers, for instance, had purchased their machinery before leaving Rhode Island. Later Pendleton and Bivingsville, the two largest Piedmont factories, secured their equipment from Paterson, New Jersey. The problem of wagon transport from Columbia or Augusta left much to be desired, and several entrepreneurs partially eliminated that difficulty by making some of their machinery.[34] All proprietors depended on water power to drive their machinery.

The proprietors marketed their products either at the factory itself, through peddlers, or through commission merchants. Most of their yarn and cloth seems to have been consumed locally, but some went to the low country, western North Carolina, and even as far away as East Tennessee, where it was bartered for flax thread, part of which was, in turn, traded to back-country shoemakers. The scarcity of specie in the Piedmont forced the factory owners to exchange yarn and cloth for all types of marketable produce.[35]

[33] Laurens Deeds, N, 72; Petition of Downs, White, and Company to General Assembly, 1836 (MS in "Public Improvements: Manufacturing" File).
[34] For examples, see Spartanburg Deeds, T, 101–102, and Greenville *Mountaineer*, September 28, 1838.
[35] Landrum, *Spartanburg County*, 162. See invoices of Hill and Clark (MSS in August Kohn Papers).

As for their labor supply, John E. Colhoun was the only back-country textile mill owner to employ Negroes, though nearly all the other manufacturers owned slaves. At one time Colhoun used nine slaves, including children, to run his factory.[36] Usually from ten to twenty-five hands were needed to operate a plant; only Pendleton and Bivingsville employed more. The workers were mainly recruited from nearby white farm families, while overseers, machinists, and skilled operatives came from the North. The Weavers, the Hills, Bates, Hutchings, Elliot, Henry, and Kershaw were examples of the Northern influx. Quite naturally, after a few years native South Carolinians, with some from North Carolina, too, began to take over the managerial positions.

Several extant contracts between Hill and Clark and their workers reveal much information about hours, wages, and factory discipline. In 1822 they hired John Craig for one year to weave or do other work at their factory "from Sunrise to Sunset" every "Lawful Day" for one dollar per day. They, in turn, agreed to furnish him a home and to employ his children. Craig's pay was to be one-third in cash and two-thirds in cotton yarn and other supplies. During the same period Hill and Clark hired two children of Vincent Willson, paying them $1.37½ per week each. The contract also stipulated that should the overseer choose to work them in the evenings, the wages for each would be 12½ cents extra per week. Payment was to be made at the end of the year, with forfeiture of wages for any time lost due to "unfaithfulness or neglect." [37]

Later labor contracts contained modifications concerning conditions of work and mode of payment. In 1827 Hill and Clark hired five children of Theophilus Cannon. Their contract stipu-

[36] Commonplace Book of John E. Colhoun, 26. In 1840 Josiah Kilgore owned 55 slaves; Vardry McBee, 24; Philip C. Lester, 13; John Weaver, 6; Leonard Hill, 6; James E. Henry, 7; H. J. Dean, 8; James Bivings, 19; David Dantzler, 21; Simpson Bobo, 5; James Nesbitt, 7; and E. C. Leitner, 5. See Sixth U. S. Census, Population, South Carolina: Greenville and Spartanburg districts (MSS in National Archives).

[37] Contracts dated February 21, 22, 1822 (MSS in August Kohn Papers).

lated that night work was not to exceed six months per year; wages, all in trade, were to be paid monthly. Hill and Clark were also to furnish Cannon with a house and a garden plot. Four contracts, in 1829, covering nine children reveal that Hill and Clark had a new policy on absenteeism. For each day a worker missed without proper excuse from the overseer, he would forfeit two days' wages, but this was not to be imposed in the case of illness. The proprietors furnished houses for three families and paid weekly wages varying from $1.37½ to $1.50 per worker. In the case of one boy whose family was not furnished living quarters, the wage was $2.00 per week.[38]

For an overseer of their cotton mill Hill and Clark signed a three-year contract with William Bates in 1827 for $1.50 per day plus living quarters. They agreed to pay Bates in cash at the end of the second and third years. At Pendleton, Colhoun contracted to pay Thomas Elliot $500 per year to superintend his woolen factory. How faithfully the manufacturers executed these contracts with their employees is a matter for conjecture. But the frequency of financial distress which afflicted some proprietors indicates that the workers suffered also. William Bates reputedly worked two years for the Weavers without pay.[39]

Despite the welter of shoestring operations, financial disasters, changes in ownership, and ruinous fires, ten back-country textile firms were still operating in 1840. The amount of capital invested varied widely in each case. For instance, John Colhoun estimated that the machinery for a small factory—consisting of two frames of 48 spindles each, two cards, a drawing frame, a roving frame, two power looms, and the necessary spools, bobbins, and yarn containers—would cost $1,221. In 1830 he valued his mill at $4,000,[40] a figure which undoubtedly included buildings. That same year, however, William Bates purchased John Weaver's factory and 230 acres of land at a sheriff's sale for a

[38] January 26, 1827, January 10, 1829, February 5, 1829, *ibid.*
[39] September 17, 1827, *ibid.*; Commonplace Book of John E. Colhoun, 26; Kennedy, *Spartanburg County*, 76–77.
[40] Commonplace Book of John E. Colhoun, 26.

paltry $1,235, considerably less than the property was worth. The capitalization of most factories varied from $5,000 to $20,000, with the figures often including commissaries, grist and saw mills, houses for workers, and other buildings. The two largest concerns in 1840, Bivingsville (1,200 spindles) and Pendleton (1,308 spindles ?) were capitalized at $63,200 and $68,000 respectively. Their actual value was probably about one-third less. The total capitalization of the ten back-country factories was about $190,000 and their spindle power 5,600.[41] The industry though small seemed securely established. Meanwhile, in 1828, the textiles industry began to revive in middle and lower South Carolina also.

[41] *Compendium of the Enumeration of the Inhabitants and Statistics of the United States, as Obtained, at the Department of State, from the Returns of the Sixth Census, by Counties and Principal Towns, Exhibiting the Population, Wealth, and Resources of the Country* (Washington, 1841), 196, with estimated corrections for errors. For example, the Pendleton Manufacturing Company began operations in 1838 with 960 spindles. The census of 1860 listed it as having 800 spindles. It is probable that the census of 1840 erred in listing it as having 1,308.

Chapter 3 Middle & Lower State Developers

The years 1815 through 1818 brought prosperity to the South Carolina cotton planter. But during these same years the few cotton mills which had survived the War of 1812 closed down. Apparently the entrepreneurs preferred instead to concentrate their efforts on cotton growing. In general, a spirit of nationalism prevailed within the state, and most of the South Carolina congressional delegation supported the Tariff Act of 1816. The tariff was not popular in South Carolina, but, in the midst of agricultural prosperity, it seemed to impose no particular burden. Besides, some believed the tariff might encourage industry within the state, a hope soon to be abandoned.

The golden agricultural era was short-lived. The Panic of 1819 caused short-staple cotton prices to fall from 29 to 34 cents a pound on the Charleston market in May, 1818, to 13 to 18 cents in May, 1819. Cotton did not rise again above 20 cents until the spring of 1825, when it reached 32 cents. In 1826 there was another significant decline in the price of the white staple. It sold for 8 to 11½ cents per pound in May. For the next six years short-staple cotton rarely brought more than 11 cents per pound.[1] Accompanying the decline in the price of cotton was the emerging concern over the protection of slavery, increasing soil exhaustion in the state, the loss of population to the West, the decrease in commerce, and the increase in tariff protection for manufacturers. By 1820 South Carolina had turned almost solidly against the tariff; by 1825 its leading politicians had turned away from nationalism to sectionalism.

With the enactment in 1828 of the "Tariff of Abominations" the more radical politicians in South Carolina began to advocate defiance of the national government, some even proposing seces-

---

[1] Alfred Glaze Smith, Jr., *Economic Readjustment of an Old Cotton State: South Carolina, 1820–1860* (Columbia, S.C., 1958), 220–21.

sion. Their wrath was momentarily calmed by Jackson's eleva-
tion to the presidency, for it was widely believed that "Old
Andy" was sympathetic with the low tariff views prevailing
in South Carolina. To the great disappointment of the Palmetto
cotton planters, the Tariff Act of 1832 brought little relief. Immediately, the radicals prepared for battle. Meanwhile, however, John C. Calhoun had brought forth his doctrine of nullification—a way to safeguard the state's interest without resort to
more drastic action—so he thought. A state convention, hastily
called by the legislature, readily endorsed Calhoun's doctrine by
nullifying the Tariff Acts of 1828 and 1832. (While the Nullifiers breathed defiance, a Unionist minority prepared to support
President Jackson by force of arms if need be.) But Henry
Clay, who wrote a compromise tariff bill, not only averted a
possible clash between national and state authorities, but he also
may well have prevented bloodshed between the Nullifiers and
the Unionists within South Carolina.[2]

   It is difficult to determine the effect that political agitation
against the tariff had upon manufacturing in the state. Congressman George McDuffie, for example, in 1828 threatened the pro-
tectionists with the prospects of a Southern industrial complex to
compete with that of the North. Yet, two years later he publicly
declared that the people of the South could not manufacture,
that slavery would not permit such an experiment.[3] However,
McDuffie himself shortly became an investor in manufacturing.
Professor Chauncey S. Boucher has concluded that "the people
of the state had become so hostile to the tariff and the manufacturing interests which demanded it, that by 1831 it was considered a great disgrace to be accused of wishing good fortune to
any manufacturing enterprise." He cited the case of Colonel

   [2] For economic aspects see *ibid.*, 1–18. For political changes see William
W. Freehling, *Prelude to Civil War: The Nullification Controversy in
South Carolina, 1816–1836* (New York and London, 1965). South Carolinians who opposed secession in 1860 were also called Unionists and came
mainly from the same sections and classes as did the Unionists of the 1830's.
   [3] David F. Houston, *A Critical Study of Nullification in South Carolina*
(New York, 1896), 41.

Table 1

Short-Staple Cotton Prices in
the Charleston Market During the Month
of May, 1815–1860

Year	Cents per pound	Year	Cents per pound	Year	Cents per pound
1815	16 −18	1830	9½–10¾	1845	5⅝– 6¾
1816	28 −31¼	1831	6½– 9½	1846	7 – 8
1817	27 −30	1832	9¾–10½	1847	11¼–12¼
1818	29 −34	1833	10 −11½	1848	5½– 6½
1819	13 −18	1834	11½–13	1849	6½– 7⅜
1820	15 −17½	1835	16¾–19	1850	11½–12
1821	10 −15½	1836	17 −20	1851	8½–10
1822	13 −17½	1837	8 −10	1852	8¾– 9½
1823	9 −12	1838	9 −11½	1853	9⅞–10½
1824	14 −16	1839	14¾–16¾	1854	8¾– 9½
1825	24 −32	1840	8 – 9	1855	9 −10⅞
1826	8 −11½	1841	10 −11½	1856	10⅜–11⅜
1827	8 −10	1842	8½–10	1857	13¾–14
1828	9 −11	1843	5½– 7	1858	12¼–12½
1829	7¾– 9¾	1844	6¾– 8	1859	10⅜–12⅛
				1860	11 −11¾

Source: Smith, *Economic Readjustment of an Old Cotton State*, 220–23.

James Chesnut's political opponent seeking to discredit Chesnut's pro-tariff position because of his investment in David R. Williams' cotton mill. A similar charge was made against William C. Preston, whose brother John S. Preston had industrial investments.[4]

Boucher's statement needs modification. Industrial development in South Carolina from 1828 to 1839 clearly indicated there was considerable support for manufacturing. The opposition

[4] Chauncey S. Boucher, "The Ante-Bellum Attitude of South Carolina toward Manufacturing and Agriculture," *Washington University Studies* (St. Louis), III (April, 1916), 243–70.

to manufacturing, to the extent that it existed, was centered almost wholly among the Nullifiers. Many Union party leaders were directly involved in promoting industry. The back-country districts with their small cotton mills, iron foundries, and live-at-home economy were Unionist strongholds. There was also much Unionist sentiment among Charleston merchants and manufacturers. Many of the Unionists later joined the Whig party, albeit that party was never strong in South Carolina. Additionally, several influential South Carolina newspapers expressed pro-manufacturing sentiment, although there was no great fanfare until the 1840's.[5] Did the Nullification furor noticeably retard industry in South Carolina? Apparently it did not, for when compared with its neighbors, South Carolina's industrial growth in the 1830's seemed to be normal. It must be remembered that while Nullification was strong in South Carolina, it was weak in North Carolina and Georgia. Politics notwithstanding, hard times caused a few low-country planters and merchants to turn to industry to try to relieve the pinch of the depressed market prices. Between 1828 and 1840 seven textile mills were established in central and lower South Carolina, six of which were still in operation at the latter date.

The first factory to open, as previously mentioned, was that of former Governor David R. Williams of Society Hill. With William Matthews he had run a cotton mill during the War of 1812 but had closed it afterwards because it was more profitable

[5] A partial list of newspapers includes the Charleston *Courier*, March 4, 1828, August 31, 1831; Columbia *Telescope*, June 12, 1829, April 30, 1830; Camden *Journal*, July 12, 1828; and Pendleton *Messenger*, May 6, 1829. Two Nullifier leaders later known to be investors in manufacturing were Governor James H. Hammond and Congressman Franklin H. Elmore. Among Unionist leaders interested in manufacturing were Greenville editor Benjamin F. Perry, Governors Richard I. Manning, Thomas Bennett, J. P. Richardson, R. F. W. Allston, and David R. Williams, Judge John B. O'Neall, Senator James Chesnut, Charleston *Courier* editor Richard Yeadon, and nearly all the Spartanburg District politicians. For a brief survey of South Carolina's antebellum industrial growth see Ernest M. Lander, Jr., "Manufacturing in South Carolina, 1815–60," *Business History Review*, XXVIII (March, 1954), 59–66.

to employ his slaves in cotton growing than in cotton manufacturing.[6] Aided by three new partners, Williams and Matthews resumed operations in 1828 under the name of the Union Manufacturing Company of South Carolina, and by the following spring the company was advertising yarn, twine, osnaburgs, and cotton bagging. In December, 1829, Williams reported that the spinning was profitable and the manufacture of woolens looked promising.[7]

Investing $5,000 in the enterprise, Williams owned 50 percent of the stock, while the remainder was divided equally among Matthews and the new partners, Simon Magwood, James Chesnut, and a man named Hunt. Magwood had been previously associated with the South Carolina Homespun Company, and Chesnut was a young planter and a rising political leader who later became a United States Senator. In an effort to attract more capital, the partners agreed to let additional investors enter the partnership on the same footing as the original five, but the results were disheartening. After carefully canvassing the possibilities, Williams informed Chesnut that there was no one else to help them, for "the merchants have been tried; they like everyone else have no fancy for enterprise that way; while the rest of the community have no funds available 'to sport' with." [8]

Failing to secure new investors, Williams adopted the policy of trying to persuade his partners to increase their investments. He told them that they should add five hundred spindles, two drawing frames, two speeders, and twelve cards if they wished to operate the plant on the most efficient basis. He added that this outlay, at a cost of over $5,000, would be sufficient to permit the profitable hiring of two overseers acquainted with all fac-

[6] Robert Mills, *Statistics of South Carolina*, 515–16.

[7] David R. Williams to James Chesnut, November 2, 1828, December 27, 1829, in David R. Williams Papers, South Caroliniana Library, University of South Carolina; Columbia *Telescope*, March 27, 1829.

[8] Williams to Chesnut, November 2, 16, 1828, in David R. Williams Papers. On October 26, 1828, Williams wrote Chesnut: "It is strange that there are so few people willing to trust their money on *faith* while, such countless millions do their souls."

ets of the business. In this manner the mill could continue to operate in the event that one of the overseers became ill or incapacitated in any way. Although he owned 50 percent of the stock, Williams did not try to force his views upon his partners. He wrote Chesnut, "We vote as a jury, all or no decision." [9]

Williams' elaborate program failed to materialize, however, as some of the stockholders apparently voted against it, and nothing further was accomplished to strengthen the company before his untimely death in November, 1830. [10] His son John inherited his share of the factory and, having already acquired some experience in the management of its operations, he immediately took over.

During the next five years Magwood, Hunt, and Matthews sold their interests, leaving the mill to John Williams, the majority stockholder, James Chesnut, and the superintendent who was named Hopkins. Chesnut also contemplated relinquishing his share in the company, but Williams earnestly entreated him to remain in the partnership. He stated that the concern had paid all its debts, had purchased $3,000 worth of machinery since 1833, and would pay a dividend of $2,193, to be divided among the three owners as soon as all the accounts due were paid in. He reminded him that the money Chesnut received from having his Negro slaves work in the factory was greater than the income would be if they merely labored on the plantation. He also pointed out that $1,200—the approximate value of Chesnut's original share—invested at 7 percent would bring only $84 per year. Williams optimistically concluded that the $400 dividend "pretty certainly" to be paid would give his partner a better business income than could be derived from any planting east of the Red River.[11] However, by 1840—just five years after his enthusiastic appraisal—the factory in full operation still only

[9] The factory began operations with $2,000 worth of machinery installed and another $859 worth enroute from Rhode Island. Williams to Chesnut, October 26, 1828, December 27, 1829, in David R. Williams Papers.

[10] General Williams was fatally injured in an accident while repairing a bridge. See Cook, *The Life and Legacy of David Rogerson Williams*, 281–85.

[11] John N. Williams to Chesnut, February 14, March 12, 1835, in David R. Williams Papers.

employed twenty-five workers to man its 700 spindles. This could be attributed to some extent to the fact that managing the plant was just a part-time job for Williams. The busy planter-industrialist, who owned more than 300 slaves, also supervised another factory at Marlboro and several large plantations.[12]

In the autumn of 1828, about the same time that David R. Williams was reorganizing his Society Hill factory, Christian Breithaupt toured Northern manufacturing centers in search of machinery and workers for a proposed cotton mill to be built in Edgefield District. Unable to procure what he desired, Breithaupt, upon the recommendation of some experienced manufacturers, hired several mechanics to come south and make the machinery on the location.[13]

Joined by Richard Cunningham, of Abbeville District, and Paul Fitzsimmons, Breithaupt erected a factory at Vaucluse on Horse Creek. The main structure was a four-story building, with the first floor of granite and the remainder of wood. The proprietors equipped the mill with 588 spindles, 10 cards, 7 power looms, and other machinery, all of which was adapted to the manufacture of cotton bagging and other coarse fabrics. They also built a village for the workers, a gristmill, and a sawmill.[14]

As the first partnership was due to expire on January 1, 1831, the proprietors decided to sell the establishment with its 1,200 acres to the highest bidder on December 20. Thomas Higginbottom and Daniel P. Merriam of North Adams, Massachusetts, bought the enterprise for $15,000. They paid only $1,000 in cash, and mortgaged the property to Breithaupt for the remaining $14,000.[15]

The new owners had held the factory but a few months when a Negro slave purposely set fire to it. One account of the fire stated that the Negro was motivated by revenge for pre-

---

[12] *Carolina Planter* (Columbia), July 22, 1840; *Compendium of the Sixth Census*, 196; Sixth U.S. Census, Population South Carolina, Darlington District (MS in National Archives).

[13] *Niles' Weekly Register*, XXXV (October 25, 1828), 136.

[14] Charleston *Courier*, July 9, September 15, November 22, 1830.

[15] *Ibid.*, November 22, 1830, January 7, 1831; Edgefield Deeds, Book 45, pp. 461–62.

viously having been accused of theft at the mill; according to a
much later version, he was trying to cover up a theft committed
at the time he burned the building. Be that as it may, the factory
was a complete loss, with the insurance covering only about one-
half of the loss.[16] Higginbottom and Merriam began the construction of a new building in 1832 but lacked sufficient funds
to complete the job and meet their financial obligations. The next
year they resold the property to Christian Breithaupt for
$7,000. [17]

Breithaupt immediately organized a new company and within
a short time secured investments totaling $52,000. The chief
backers were Congressman George McDuffie, who invested
$10,000; Mitchell King, a prominent Charleston banker and
merchant, $5,000; a Mr. Seabrook of Edisto Island, $5,000; a
man named St. John of Augusta, $5,000; his two former partners,
Richard Cunningham and Paul Fitzsimmons, $5,000 each; and
Breithaupt, himself, who put in $10,000. [18] In December, 1833,
the General Assembly incorporated the Vaucluse Manufacturing Company with capital not to exceed $100,000. It was the
first textile establishment to be chartered by the state of South
Carolina since the South Carolina Homespun Company in 1808.
The new factory building was a five-story granite structure
which measured 40 by 100 feet (part of its foundation is still in
use) and was equipped with 1,800 spindles and 35 looms. Fifty
workers were employed at the mill.[19]

George McDuffie was elected president of the company but
was soon too busy with his new duties as governor to give the
mill proper attention. The board of directors seldom met, and

[16] The fire occurred July 22, 1831. The slave confessed and was sentenced
to die by a local court. Pendleton *Messenger*, August 3, 1831. A brief and
generally accurate history of Vaucluse was written by "Benardo" in the
Charleston *Daily Courier*, January 6, 1860.

[17] Deed dated October 4, 1833 (MS in vault of the Graniteville Company,
Graniteville, S.C.).

[18] Charleston *Daily Courier*, January 6, 1860; William Gregg, "Southern
Patronage to Southern Imports and Southern Industry," *De Bow's Review*,
XXIX (October, 1860), 494.

[19] Charleston *Courier*, November 23, 1836, September 5, 1837.

Breithaupt's death in December, 1835, removed the one capable person who had actively been engaged in supervising the business. McDuffie tendered his resignation in early 1837, but by that time the company's affairs had fallen into a state of incredible neglect. McDuffie advised the stockholders to meet on March 20 to create a government for the company as none existed.[20]

Following McDuffie's advice, the stockholders elected a new president, James G. O. Wilkinson, but entrusted the active management of the factory to a new investor, William Gregg, a former jeweler from Columbia. According to Gregg, the deplorable condition of the enterprise not only included a debt of $6,000 but even worse, an ignorant superintendent who "had never before had charge, even of a single department of a mill." [21] Yet, within a few months Gregg announced that the factory was turning out eight thousand yards of osnaburgs and linseys per week. A few weeks later he presented the stockholders with an accounting which showed the debt had been paid and that a surplus of $5,000 had been accumulated. The statement boosted somewhat the value of the depreciated stock, and on December 30, 1837, the company, at Gregg's suggestion, sold out to George McDuffie and John Bauskett for $33,000. [22]

Shortly afterwards Bauskett, an Edgefield lawyer, planter, and state senator, bought McDuffie's interest. In September, 1838, he wrote that he was "anxiously engaged" in manufacturing at Vaucluse, which he had purchased on credit and expected to pay for out of future profits. It was producing a greater income than his plantation, he said, but was so time consuming that he had to

20 David D. Wallace, "A Hundred Years of William Gregg and Graniteville" (Typescript in Gregg Foundation Files, Graniteville Company), 19–20; George McDuffie to John Bauskett, February 25, 1837, in Thomas P. Martin, ed., "The Advent of William Gregg and the Graniteville Company," *Journal of Southern History*, XI (August, 1945), 402.
21 William Gregg, *Essays on Domestic Industry: or, an Enquiry into the Expediency of Establishing Cotton Manufactures in South Carolina* (Charleston, S.C., 1845), 33–34.
22 *Ibid.*; Charleston *Courier*, October 16, 1837; deed from J. G. O. Wilkinson to McDuffie and Bauskett (MS in vault of the Graniteville Company).

give up his practice of law.[23] Bauskett increased the number of spindles at Vaucluse to two thousand and the number of laborers, nearly all of whom were white, to seventy. In 1840 the value of the plant's production was worth $60,000 per year on an investment valued at only $40,000.[24]

In 1834 a group of thirty entrepreneurs bought the mill site at Beard's Falls on the Saluda River two miles from Columbia. Under the name of the Saluda Manufacturing Company they began the construction of the largest cotton mill yet attempted in South Carolina. The legislature immediately incorporated the company with a capital stock of $60,000 and the privilege of extending it to $500,000. The corporation's president was David Ewart; the other directors were Thomas Wells, John J. Gracey, John G. Brown, and Shubal Blanding. Of the remaining stockholders, the most prominent were Judge John Belton O'Neall, Franklin H. Elmore, and Congressman James H. Hammond. Most of the investors were either Columbia businessmen or nearby planters.[25]

The Saluda Manufacturing Company built an impressive looking establishment. Its main structure was a large granite building, 200 by 45 feet, consisting of four stories and an attic. Nearby stood a granite picker house, wooden sizing and drying houses, a blacksmith shop for building and repairing machinery, a sawmill, a boarding house for the white operatives, cabins for the Negroes, a commissary, a warehouse, and a hotel. The dam and

[23] John Bauskett to Mrs. Ann Wadlington, September 25, 1838, in Thomas Wadlington Papers (Photostatic copies in Duke University Library).

[24] *Compendium of the Sixth Census*, 196; Charleston *Courier*, June 28, 1841. The census figure of $70,000 capital value for Vaucluse is too high. Bauskett and McDuffie bought the mill for $33,000 in 1837 and Bauskett sold one-half interest in it for $20,000 in 1841. Edgefield Deeds, CCC, 30–32. In 1839 Bauskett reported the factory was manufacturing 1,100 yards of cloth and 150 pounds of yarn per day. John Bauskett to Thomas Bauskett, April 19, 1839, in Thomas Wadlington Papers.

[25] Petition of the Saluda Manufacturing Company stockholders to General Assembly, 1834 (MS in "Public Improvements: Manufacturing" File); Edwin J. Scott, *Random Recollections of a Long Life, 1806–1876* (Columbia, S.C., 1884), 44–45, 69–70.

millrace furnished a 16-foot head of water to turn the two water-wheels, which were eighteen feet in diameter by eighteen feet wide.[26] The ruins of the dam may be seen today from Highway I-26 on the outskirts of Columbia.

William Gregg later stated that the Saluda Manufacturing Company started "with most brilliant prospects" but made the error of trying to operate on too large a scale for the amount of capital at its command. In New England a company would have sought to raise $400,000 before establishing a factory as large as that which the Saluda stockholders had envisioned. Consequently, for several years the corporation eked out a "sickly existence." [27]

A lack of faith in the company's ultimate success was shown by investor James H. Hammond and his Columbia adviser Pierce M. Butler. Butler wrote on June 23, 1834: "A call is made upon you for $15 a share on your cotton Factory stock. . . . The amt. will be $150—Shall I pay it for you; I will do so with pleasure. I believe there are no purchasers—you can get $30 for the $50 you paid & quit if you wish; but you might & most probably would injure the Stock & create prejudice against you. I dont like the yankee concern—but I expect you had best Stick to a bad bargain to the extent of your $1,000." Hammond completed payment of his stock subscription the following year, and Butler then advised him to sell, pointing out that it was likely Hammond would have "additional cost for 2 years longer at least—before a dividend." In June Hammond sold at a loss, but Butler thought it well that he did, for the stock was under par "& will keep getting worse." [28]

In an effort to acquire more capital the company decided to reopen the subscription books and take in new stockholders. David Ewart announced on February 18, 1837, that an additional $100,000 would be offered to the public at $100 per share, with

[26] Charleston *Courier*, September 3, 1839.
[27] William Gregg, "Southern Patronage to Southern Imports and Southern Industry," 229; William Gregg, "Practical Results of Southern Manufactures," *De Bow's Review*, XVIII (June, 1855), 787.
[28] Pierce M. Butler to James H. Hammond, June 23, 1834, April 4, June 11, 29, 1835, in Hammond Papers, South Caroliniana Library.

$10 payable in cash and the balance in bimonthly installments of $10 per share. He informed the public that the mill was one-fourth filled with machinery and that another fourth was being set up at that time. By December, 1837, the plant had four thousand spindles and sixty-four looms in operation.[29] But the company's effort to secure additional capital was disappointing; hence, the board of directors applied to the legislature for a loan of $50,000 for four years. They asserted that although $120,000 had already been invested, they thought it would be advantageous to expand operations (evidently meaning to finish equipping the factory with machinery). The present stockholders, they added, lacked the additional capital to fulfill their plan. The Senate was favorably disposed to aid the corporation, but the House defeated the motion. Thwarted in their fund raising endeavors, the stockholders two years later decided to sell their sixty-four slaves and their partially equipped establishment at public auction. Ewart, with an eye toward a more profitable sale, cleverly stressed the importance of the forthcoming railroad to Columbia.[30]

In December, 1839, a new organization with a new but similar name, the Saluda Company, bought the buildings, machinery, and land for $60,100. The old company also auctioned its slaves at an average price of $600, but reports of the transaction did not state how many, if any, of the Negroes were purchased by the new company. The Saluda Company was composed of twelve stockholders, only one of whom, Judge John Belton O'Neall, had been an original stockholder in the old Saluda Manufacturing Company. Among the new investors were John and Edward H. Fisher, operators of a small yarn mill of their own, and the scientist and scholar Dr. Robert W. Gibbes. With Edward H. Fisher as its agent, the company announced the con-

29 Charleston *Courier*, February 18, December 11, 1837.
30 Petition of the Saluda Manufacturing Company to General Assembly, 1837 (MS in "Public Improvements: Manufacturing" File); House Journals, 1837 (MS in South Carolina Department of Archives and History), 143, 150, 161; Charleston *Courier*, September 3, 1839.

tinued manufacture of shirtings, osnaburgs, and yarn. By this time the value of its annual production was slightly over $100,000. [31]

Two other cotton mills which began operations in the early 1830's were the Fulton factory in lower Sumter District and the Fishers' mill at Dent's Pond, a few miles east of Columbia. In November, 1830, a visitor in the region of Fulton Post Office described a three-story brick and stone building recently erected for use as a cotton mill. The proprietor, Jeptha Dyson, apparently was financed in his undertaking by two neighboring planters, future Governor John P. Richardson and former Governor Richard I. Manning. How quickly he began operation cannot be determined, but at least as early as March, 1832, agents were offering "Fulton Factory Yarn" for sale. In 1840 Dyson's factory, equipped with 1,056 spindles, was annually producing $19,000 worth of goods. He employed about twenty-five hands, most of whom were slaves.[32]

The history of the Fisher brothers' mill is obscure, but it is known to have been in operation as early as 1833. At that time E. H. Fisher advertised that the factory was "in full operation" and that yarn of different sizes was for sale. After their investment in the Saluda factory the Fishers evidently abandoned their mill at Dent's Pond.[33]

In 1836 John McQueen, later a United States Congressman, John N. Williams, chief investor in the Society Hill factory, and William T. Ellerbe formed a partnership to build a cotton mill

[31] Lexington Deeds, M, 99; Camden *Journal*, December 21, 1839; *Carolina Planter* (Columbia), August 5, 1840; *Compendium of the Sixth Census*, 196.
[32] Charleston *Courier*, November 3, 1830; Camden *Journal*, March 3, 1832; *Compendium of the Sixth Census*, 196; Sixth U. S. Census, Population, South Carolina: Sumter District (MS in National Archives). Manning and Richardson endorsed Dyson's note for $7,000 and loaned him an additional $18,500, for which he mortgaged his 800 acre plantation and 30 slaves. Sumter Deeds, HH, 262–65.
[33] Columbia *Telescope*, December 13, 1833; Scott, *Random Recollections*, 44–45. The plant was not listed in the 1840 census returns. The Fishers possibly moved their machinery to the Saluda mill.

near Bennettsville in Marlboro District. Together they secured three adjoining tracts of land totaling approximately one thousand acres and constructed a three-story wooden factory building, a sawmill, a gristmill, dwellings for the hands, and other necessary storehouses and shops. With two thousand spindles and thirty-six looms the Marlboro factory began operations in 1838. The total cost of the enterprise was $37,000. [34]

After a visit to the mill in 1840 Dr. Robert W. Gibbes reported that it manufactured three to four thousand yards of cotton cloth per week besides spinning six hundred pounds of yarn. He credited John N. Williams with being the principal director of the factory, which he said was "one of the neatest and best ordered, (although worked by negroes,) that it has been our lot to visit." [35]

A last example of the early type of textile milling is that which Burwell Boykin, Thomas Lang, and William Anderson organized at Camden under the name of William Anderson and Company. The partners paid Lang $8,000 for 620 acres of land on Pine Tree Creek. The property included a flour mill, a dam, and a mill pond. At this site they constructed a wooden factory building, equipped it with one thousand spindles, and began operations in 1838. They also built a village for their workers, who numbered about fifty in 1840. [36]

In 1840 the respective labor forces of the middle and lower South Carolina textile mills varied from twenty-five each for Society Hill and Fulton to 111 for Saluda. With the possible exception of the Fishers all concerns used slave labor to some extent. In 1836 Vaucluse was employing thirty whites and twenty slaves. Three years later the Saluda Manufacturing Company advertised sixty-four trained Negro operatives for sale. Jeptha Dyson and David R. Williams trained their plantation hands to operate textile machinery.

[34] Marlboro Deeds, O, 260–61, 461–63, Q, 150–52; Charleston *Courier*, March 24, 1842.
[35] *Carolina Planter* (Columbia), July 22, 1840.
[36] Kershaw Deeds, O, 90–91; Camden *Journal*, June 30, 1849; *Compendium of the Sixth Census*, 196.

In a letter to James Chesnut, written on November 16, 1828, Williams outlined his program to utilize slaves in the factory. Negroes unsuited for field work would be trained as weavers if they showed an aptitude for this type of work. The little children, who were unfit for weaving, would quill the looms, do piecing, and perform other routine chores. Meanwhile the young women would do the carding and spinning. When a child became large enough to be worth $20 a year as a plantation worker, he or she would be exchanged for a younger one—except in cases where some extraordinary talent for textile work was displayed. Williams told Chesnut that Hopkins, the overseer, was satisfied that he could "learn our negroes and large ones too at the simplest or first—processes, quicker than . . . any white children he has ever had under him in New England." An old man, six children, and six young women were already at work, Williams said, and more would be needed when additional machinery arrived. He therefore asked Chesnut to send such "little homony eaters" as he pleased, taking care to include an older person to wash and mend their clothes. As his parting advice, Williams requested Chesnut to instruct the Negroes that they would all fare alike and "must conform to orders." Two months later he informed Chesnut that an additional eleven slave children and women had reached the factory. He put them together in a house containing two large bedrooms and a hall with a fireplace. The children were under the care of a slave woman, who stayed with them at night and accompanied them to the factory during the day. Another Negro woman cooked for the entire household.

At first Williams boasted of the healthfulness and fecundity of the factory location: there had been many births and no deaths among the slaves. A year later, however, he changed his tune, admitting that the health of the workers, and also of the overseer Hopkins, gave him anxiety. Some of the workers had had measles; nevertheless, he believed that the work would progress nicely unless Hopkins became ill.

According to Williams' estimate in October, 1828, the factory would need ten little Negroes too small to work in the fields, five young women to spin and wind, two cooks, one clerk, one laborer, one spinning overseer, and one "filer." For wages he expected to allow $25 per year for each child, $75 for each woman spinner or winder, $300 for the clerk and $700 for the master spinner. He would hire weavers at five cents per yard. Later he hired a clerk for $204 a year and three Negroes for $20 per month. The system not only made use of slaves, some of whom might have been otherwise unproductive, but it also tended to eliminate considerable cash expense.[37]

Many of the slave laborers at Vaucluse also belonged to stockholders. George McDuffie, for example, hired out seven of his Negroes to the corporation. When he resigned as president, he offered to permit five of them to remain with the company for $700 per year. For two others, a carpenter and his wife, he asked $300, vigorously maintaining that he could hire out the carpenter alone for a dollar a day.[38]

The middle and low country mills produced a greater variety of products than the textile plants in the Piedmont, and William Gregg severely criticized them for such diversity. He said that Vaucluse introduced such complicated machinery "as to render it impossible for it to produce profit, except by the nicest and most skilful management." [39] David R. Williams manufactured osnaburgs, shirting, bale rope, sewing thread, Negro woolen cloth, twine, coarse yarn, and cotton bagging. Vaucluse made bagging, yarn, osnaburgs, linseys, and woolen cloth, while Saluda produced bagging, shirting, yarn, and osnaburgs.[40] The Marlboro, DeKalb, Fishers, and Fulton mills did not manufacture

[37] David R. Williams to James Chesnut, October 26, November 16, 1828, January 18, December 27, 1829, May 14, 1830, and John N. Williams to Chesnut, February 14, 1835, in David R. Williams Papers; David R. Williams to Chesnut, August, 1829, cited in Cook, *David Rogerson Williams*, 144–45.

[38] McDuffie to John Bauskett, February 25, 1837, in Martin, "The Advent of Gregg and Graniteville," 402.

[39] Gregg, *Domestic Industry*, 33.

[40] Columbia *Telescope*, March 27, 1829; Charleston *Courier*, September 15, 1830, September 5, October 16, 1837; *South-Carolinian* (Columbia), November 10, 1842.

so wide a variety. Whereas the upstate mills seemed to concentrate on yarn, the middle and low state plants leaned to osnaburgs and other types of plantation clothing. On one occasion John Bauskett wrote from Vaucluse that his osnaburgs found a ready market but that his yarn, though made in much smaller quantities, moved slowly.[41]

The problem of effective marketing was of great concern to all of the textile manufacturers. Although some goods were sent North, by and large the cotton mill proprietors depended on local markets prior to 1840. On that score Gregg singled out Vaucluse and Saluda as examples of managerial shortsightedness. He insisted that the factories should go after distant, as well as local, customers.[42] Most of the companies established agencies at the factory and employed merchants in nearby towns to sell their products on commission. These agents advertised frequently in the local newspapers, and they spoke of their cloth and yarn in glowing terms. Nor did they hesitate to berate a Northern competitor. Jasper Gibbs, agent for Vaucluse in 1836, advertised cotton osnaburgs "of a quality admitted to be two cents superior to Lowell's No. 1, at a lower rate than that inferior fabric commanded on the Augusta market." J. T. Mickle, a Columbia merchant, advertised DeKalb yarn "to be fully equal, if not superior, to the manufacture of any other establishment." Other phrases used to attract customers included: "A complete assortment of Cotton Yarn . . . in quantities to suit, at the manufacturer's price," and "osnaburgs and yarn for sale on accommodating terms." [43]

The practice of using agents to market their products was far from satisfactory to some of the manufacturers. David Williams

[41] John Bauskett to Thomas Bauskett, April 19, 1839, in Thomas Wadlington Papers.
[42] Gregg, *Domestic Industry*, 33–34. At one time David R. Williams shipped yarn to New York City. *Niles' Weekly Register*, XXXIV (August 9, 1828), 379.
[43] Columbia *Telescope*, December 13, 1833, April 9, 1836; *South-Carolinian* (Columbia), November 10, 1842; *Southern Chronicle* (Columbia), November 12, 1840.

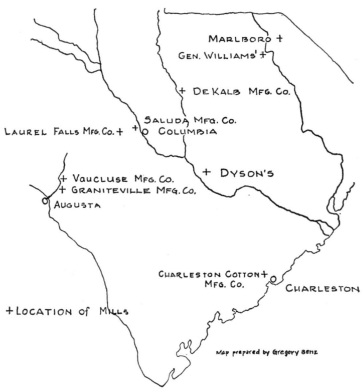

Map 2 The Middle and Lower State Textile Mills, 1840–1860.

called agents "abominable things" and regretted having to rely upon them. Gregg also disliked agencies, and in 1837, when placed in charge of Vaucluse, he announced the withdrawal of the corporation's agencies in Augusta and Hamburg. Henceforth, all merchants would be put on an equal footing, he declared. The company fixed regular prices for all its goods, by the piece or by the bale, all of which indicated a previous lack of uniformity of prices quoted by the various agents. Vaucluse offered liberal discounts and six months' credit to purchasers of five or more bales of osnaburgs. That same year Saluda announced a similar policy. It would sell at prices "regulated" by the New York market and deliver goods in Columbia or "any other place" with four months' credit to buyers of five or more bales. The price would be one cent per yard higher on smaller purchases.[44]

In an effort to increase sales some manufacturers personally went out and drummed up business among the planters. Evidence of this practice was vividly displayed in a letter from George McDuffie to John Bauskett shortly after the two had bought the Vaucluse mill. McDuffie expressed no confidence in the ability of a few Augusta merchants to market their goods. He wrote: "Our customers are the planters. I shall attend at Abbeville C.H. on sale day next expressly to make engagements, & I have no doubt I can engage 20,000 yards to be delivered & paid for by the 1st of May. Do you as much in Edgefield. Don't wait for the people to come to you. Turn out. We must live in this use of means. We shall have made ... by that time 150,000 yards of osnaburgs worth $18,000, and we must have it converted into cash. The Spring is our great harvest, for then the planters *must* have our goods." The system must have met with some success, for the following year Bauskett wrote that the osnaburgs received ready sales.[45]

One of the major difficulties the South Carolinians faced in marketing their goods was the competition of cheaper New England-made textiles. (The larger New England mills were capable of mass production.) Between 1826 and 1845 Massachusetts chartered eight cotton textile companies with authorized capital over a million dollars each. When Williams' prices were compared with those in New York, it was evident that he could not meet the competition. He sold coarse yarn from 25 to 29

[44] David R. Williams to Chesnut, December 27, 1829, in David R. Williams Papers; Gregg in the Charleston *Courier,* October 16, 1837; *Southern Times and State Gazette* (Columbia), November 28, 1837.
[45] McDuffie to Bauskett, February 3, 1838, in George McDuffie Papers, South Caroliniana Library; Bauskett to Thomas Bauskett, April 19, 1839, in Thomas Wadlington Papers.

cents per pound and his osnaburgs and shirting from 10 to 14
cents per yard. At the same time, coarse yarn was selling in New
York for 20.8 cents per pound and brown shirting for 7 cents
per yard.[46]

In addition to the differences in price, there were also differences in quality, both of which Williams readily recognized and
endeavored to eliminate. He was satisfied that Society Hill osnaburgs were of better quality than the Northern goods which
used a soft-spun filling. The New England cloth would not wear
as well as his fabric, which was woven of hard-spun yarn; yet
he admitted that the soft-spun goods looked more attractive. He
was therefore anxious to acquire some mule frames in order to
produce a similar type. He confided to Chesnut, "We must con-
sult even the whims of purchasers if we can find it out." As for
price, Williams concluded it was all important, and he wrote:
"One preference we have . . . and *one only*, they [the planters]
prefer to use *cotton* to *flax*, & therefore if they can get our osna-
burghs, at the same price as *foreign*, they will get it; on every
other consideration 99 out of every 100, go for cheapness *wholly*
[therefore] as the yankeys make theirs of *cotton* also, we may
preach, till the cows come home, about *staple* & *tariff* imposers,
etc etc; if we do not sell cheaper we shall have no preference; if
only as cheap, we stand on the same foot, with 'our brethren of
the north.' " [47]

In time the discrepancy between New York prices and those
of South Carolina manufacturers decreased perceptibly. In 1839
Bauskett sold coarse yarn for 25 cents per pound while the New
York market listed it at 22.8 cents. Three years later Saluda advertised shirting at 5 cents per yard and yarn at 16.2 cents per

[46] Columbia *Telescope*, March 23, May 8, 1829; David R. Williams to
Chesnut, May 14, 1830, in David R. Williams Papers; Victor S. Clark,
History of Manufactures in the United States, 1607-1860 (Washington,
D.C., 1916), 613; Caroline F. Ware, *The Early New England Cotton Manu-
facture*, 302.

[47] David R. Williams to Chesnut, February 10, 1830, in David R. Williams
Papers.

pound; shirting was also 5 cents per yard and yarn 15.8 cents per pound in New York.[48]

In conclusion it should be noted that in 1840 the Piedmont cotton mills outnumbered those in middle and lower South Carolina by ten to six. But the total spindle power of the latter was approximately 10,700 compared with 5,600 for the up-country establishments. Only two of the mills above the fall line housed over 1,000 spindles each, whereas only one of the middle or low state factories contained less than that. This, of course, meant that the labor force, the capital investment, and the productive capacity of the latter were much greater than those of the Piedmont factories. Another significant difference was that the upcountry mills, with one exception, used white labor exclusively, while the central and lower South Carolina mills relied mainly on slave labor. The Piedmont mills also were established in most instances by New Englanders or North Carolinians; elsewhere they were promoted by local entrepreneurs. In the overall picture the mills in the state increased from four in 1820 to sixteen in 1840, with three others having recently closed down. The period of greatest expansion was from 1828 to 1838, during which time sixteen cotton mills were constructed. The mills, with 16,300 spindles in operation in 1840, employed 570 workers, had a capital investment of $500,000, and produced $380,000 worth of cotton goods.[49]

[48] Clark, *Manufactures, 1607–1860*, p. 613; John Bauskett to Thomas Bauskett, April 19, 1839, in Thomas Wadlington Papers; *South-Carolinian* (Columbia), November 10, 1842.

[49] Based on *Compendium of the Sixth Census*, 196, with corrections for obvious discrepancies. For example, the census reported the DeKalb factory with only 120 spindles and Saluda with 5,000. DeKalb began operations in 1838 with 1,000 and Saluda possessed 3,838 when sold in December, 1839. Marlboro was reported with a capital investment of $90,000; whereas a news account two years later stated it cost $37,000, more in keeping with a 2000-spindle mill housed in a wooden building.

Chapter 4 Gregg & Graniteville

After the textile expansion of the 1830's not another cotton mill was constructed in South Carolina until 1844. From that date until 1851 about a dozen concerns were projected and eight were actually established. This pattern of growth was similar throughout the Southeast. A significant factor distinguished the textile development in the 1840's from that of the 1830's. Whereas the public had appeared disinterested and in some cases antipathetic to industry in the thirties, expansion in the forties was accompanied by considerable publicity and overwhelming newspaper support.

The awakened public interest in manufacturing was due to several reasons, not the least of which was the severe agricultural depression. As already noted, the price of short-staple cotton in Charleston had dropped from a high of 32 cents per pound in 1825 to a low of 8 cents in 1826. The market recovered somewhat in the mid-1830's, topping 20 cents per pound in 1836, but the Panic of 1837, and the subsequent depression, kept the price under 10 cents during most of the 1840's. This aroused some of the planter class from their one-crop lethargy. The need for diversification in agriculture and for increased manufacturing was voiced in 1841 by former Congressman James H. Hammond in a speech to the members of the State Agricultural Society. He concluded that South Carolina could no longer compete with the Southwest in growing cotton. The state would have to shift to other crops and develop a live-at-home economy. By fostering industry South Carolinians might retain much of the $8 million annually spent for goods elsewhere.[1]

The State Agricultural Society was generally in accord with Hammond's proposed union of agriculture and industry. As a

[1] James H. Hammond, *Anniversary Oration of the State Agricultural Society of South Carolina* (Columbia, S.C., 1841), 3–26. Hammond was elected governor of South Carolina in 1842.

matter of fact, many of its members were, or had been, associated with various manufacturing enterprises. At the 1841 session the society passed resolutions calling for the increased use of cotton in American factories and the substitution of cotton rope and baling for similar articles of hemp. At its 1844 meeting the group resolved "that a combined system of Agriculture, Manufactures, and Commerce, are essential in promoting the prosperity and happiness of a community." For several years thereafter, the society maintained its interest in manufacturing, and more than half of the speeches delivered before it during the 1840's emphasized the need for the application of science to agriculture and also increased manufacturing.[2]

Elsewhere occasional voices were raised in behalf of developing the industrial resources of the state,[3] but public sentiment did not crystallize into action until William Gregg openly became involved. Gregg, a self-made man, had accumulated a fortune in the jewelry business in such a short time that he was able to retire, financially secure, while still in his thirties. He soon became interested in textiles and acquired part ownership of Vaucluse in 1837. After the plant was sold to other stockholders in December of that year, Gregg began a serious study of textile manufacturing and traveled North to see the industry in operation there. He became firmly convinced that previous failures of Southern mills had been for the most part due to ignorance and poor supervision. He predicted that cotton manufacturing would become an important branch of business in South Carolina before many years. All that was needed, he wrote, was "for a few of our enterprising men to embark in it to render it success-

[2] Marjorie S. Mendenhall, "A History of Agriculture in South Carolina, 1790–1860" (Ph.D. dissertation, University of North Carolina, 1940), 274–76. Among the Society's members were Congressman Wilson Nesbitt, Wade Hampton, II, and J. M. Taylor, stockholders of the Nesbitt Iron Manufacturing Company; Governor James H. Hammond, Judge John B. O'Neall, Dr. Robert W. Gibbes, and W. M. Taylor, investors in Saluda; George C. Leitner, in Bivingsville; Congressman John McQueen, in Marlboro; and Governor George McDuffie, in Vaucluse.

[3] See, for instance, *Speech of Maj. James Edward Henry, on Productive Corporations.*

ful and a favourite means of investment." [4] In 1843, in partnership with his brother-in-law General James Jones, he again
became a proprietor of Vaucluse.

To propagate his ideas favoring industry, Gregg, under the
pseudonym "South Carolina," published twelve articles in the
Charleston *Courier*, September 20–December 11, 1844, and later
republished the articles in pamphlet form under his real name.
He pointed out that the state's poverty was causing its ambitious
citizens to emigrate to more productive areas. South Carolina
was needlessly dependent on other states for manufactured
articles and even agricultural products. This was due to the
state's overwhelming preoccupation with cotton, which he considered a curse rather than a blessing. "Cotton has been to South
Carolina," Gregg said, "what the Mines of Mexico were to
Spain, it has produced us such an abundant supply of all the
luxuries and elegancies of life, with so little exertion on our part,
that we have become enervated, unfitted for other and more
laborious pursuits, and unprepared to meet the state of things
which sooner or later must come about."

Gregg offered much more evidence to show that cotton manufacturing could be more profitable than cotton growing in South
Carolina. He discussed the natural advantages that the state
possessed over New England in respect to raw material, cheap
water-power sites, and a plentiful labor supply of poor whites
and slaves. In addition Southern manufacturers possessed a
potentially large market for cotton bagging and rope. He furnished detailed advice to prospective factory owners concerning
the type of mills that should be established, and he enumerated
the causes of failure of such earlier concerns as Vaucluse and
Saluda. His argument, though sometimes repetitious, was logical,
clear, and well fortified with convincing data.

Gregg was frequently given to blunt language. He castigated
Charleston businessmen for investing capital outside the state,
and he scored the politicians for their shortsightedness. The

[4] William Gregg to James H. Hammond, November 3, 1841, in Hammond Papers, South Caroliniana Library.

latter, he explained, needed to satisfy the capitalists that "we are not on the verge of revolution, but that there is safety in investments in South Carolina." At times he became painfully specific, pointing the finger of censure at Governors George McDuffie and James Hamilton and at John C. Calhoun and Langdon Cheves. Of McDuffie he asked: "Why did you permit the establishment [Vaucluse] to dwindle, sicken and die, purely from the want of attention, which you well know is essential to the success of your cotton plantation? " He criticized McDuffie again for a speech the latter had delivered in Richmond in which he fallaciously complained that a Northern manufacturer of cotton unjustly made greater profits than he did as a grower of cotton. Gregg was also convinced that the South had greatly magnified the tariff's influence as a cause of Southern poverty. He added: "I cannot see how we are to look with a reasonable hope of relief, even from its abandonment, without a total change of our habits." [5]

Gregg's articles were highly praised by numerous newspapers and widely circulated in South Carolina and neighboring states. When a Savannah paper reprinted them, the Charleston *Courier* declared that they "should be in the hands of every citizen, who desires to be enlightened as to the true interest of the South." On the other hand, Gregg drew fire from some of the politicians, as two of his letters to Calhoun indicate. In the first Gregg wrote: "I regret now that I did not, before it went to Press in pamphlet form, extract such matter from it as may be deemed offensive to our leading Politicians." In the second he added: "I am not a politician, and regret now, having made allusion in the pamphlet to the protective system, for it ought to have no connection with the subject, the remarks relative to Gen McDuffie & Mr Simmons [a Northern manufacturer] were penned in a moment of great excitement, after reading Gen McDs Richmond Speech, which I thought at the time to be full of absurdities." Gregg

[5] William Gregg, *Essays on Domestic Industry*, which also included much of the story of Gregg's earlier career. Hamilton and McDuffie served as governors of South Carolina 1830–32 and 1834–36, respectively.

followed his apology with a lengthy discussion of the opportunities for industry in the state. In his attempt to swing Calhoun behind the industrial movement, he said: "You occupy an enviable position in South Carolina, every eye is fixed on you, and much depends on your decision in this matter. We have $200,000 ready to go into cotton spinning in Charleston and only wait the action of the Legislature to obtain a charter of incorporation." [6]

In July of 1845, four articles entitled "Cotton Manufactures in the Old Atlantic Southern States" appeared in the Charleston *Courier*. These were obviously the work of Gregg, again writing under the pseudonym "South Carolina." He reiterated some of his earlier arguments in favor of manufacturing and blamed the distress of the Southeast on the overproduction of cotton. He concluded that South Carolina's salvation lay in the establishment of fifty cotton mills of seven thousand spindles each. In November Gregg followed these articles with two more which also favored liberal incorporation laws.[7]

Under the impact of agricultural distress and Gregg's convincing propaganda the local newspapers slowly awakened to the economic significance of fostering manufacturing in the state. Publications that for years had remained silent on the subject now began to editorialize in favor of home industry. During the late 1840's there seems to have been only two South Carolina papers that voiced opposition to such a program. The newspaper effort reached its peak in 1850 and 1851 and declined rapidly thereafter, due no doubt to returning agricultural prosperity. The neighboring states of North Carolina and Georgia had similar movements in the 1840's, which also declined in the early fifties, but with more tangible success than that which attended the South Carolinians' efforts.[8] In evaluating Gregg's

[6] Charleston *Courier*, February 8, 1845; Gregg to Calhoun, March 15, April, 1845, in John C. Calhoun Papers, Clemson University Library.

[7] Charleston *Courier*, November 6, 11, 1845.

[8] This writer examined approximately seventy-five South Carolina newspapers published between 1830 and 1860, in some cases scattered issues, in others complete files. An example of newspaper publicity may be noted

William Gregg of Vaucluse and Graniteville, the undisputed leader of the South Carolina antebellum textile tycoons. From an old portrait.

Three prominent antebellum textile entrepreneurs of South Carolina were, left, Gabriel Cannon, sometime lieutenant-governor of the state and a co-founder of Pacolet mill at Fingerville; center, James H. Taylor, a member of the Board of Directors of Graniteville and also agent for the Charleston Cotton Manufactory; and right, Henry Pinckney Hammett, son-in-law and partner of William Bates of Batesville.

The Saluda mill, one of the largest and earliest textile factories, as it appeared about 1860. From an old newspaper print of an early steel engraving.

Graniteville, as it appeared in 1963. Completed in 1843, it was built of granite blocks quarried from a nearby hillside.

work, Broadus Mitchell concluded: "To the extent that mills were built in the forties as a result of public agitation, William Gregg was almost wholly responsible." [9]

William Gregg not only preached the gospel of industrialization, he took practical steps to help realize it. With Otis Mills, Hiram Hutchison, Joel Smith, and others, he formulated plans to erect a large textile mill in Horse Creek Valley. Gregg, who was well acquainted with the region, tentatively selected a place about three miles below Vaucluse and within one mile of the South Carolina Railroad. He and his associates then sought a charter of incorporation. Not sure of obtaining one in South Carolina, they applied to the legislature of Georgia as well. It is believed that Gregg personally attended the session of the South Carolina legislature in December, 1845. Moreover, he saw to it that each legislator was given a copy of his recent pamphlet favoring liberal charters of incorporation. In the pamphlet he stressed the advantages of joint-stock companies in attracting small investors and noted that most manufacturing in the United States was carried on by such companies. He called attention to the South Carolina law of 1837 authorizing limited co-partnerships and said that he knew of no instance of that law being abused.[10]

---

in the Camden *Journal*, a weekly or semi-weekly sheet. It increased its items about manufacturing from an occasional one or two per year in the 1830's to a high of sixteen in 1851. In 1852 the number of such items declined to four. For a more detailed study of the movement in the 1840's, see Herbert Collins, "The Southern Industrial Gospel before 1860," *Journal of Southern History*, XII (August, 1946), 386–402. For textile developments in Georgia and North Carolina, see R. W. Griffin, "The Origins of the Industrial Revolution in Georgia: Cotton Textiles, 1810–1865," *Georgia Historical Quarterly*, XLII (December, 1958), 354–75; and Diffee W. Standard and Richard W. Griffin, "The Cotton Textile Industry in Ante-Bellum North Carolina," *North Carolina Historical Review*, XXXIV (January, 1957), 15–35, (April, 1957), 131–64.

[9] Broadus Mitchell, *The Rise of the Cotton Mills in the South* (Baltimore, 1921), 42–43.

[10] Broadus Mitchell, *William Gregg, Factory Master of the Old South* (Chapel Hill, N.C., 1928), 33–34; Charleston *Courier*, November 6, 11, 1845.

As it turned out, only the South Carolina legislature granted the associates a charter, but even this was a struggle. The House Committee on Incorporations was under the chairmanship of John Bauskett, a former Vaucluse proprietor. Oddly enough, he spoke at length against the bill and reported unfavorably for the committee. On the other side the proposed charter found two ardent champions in James E. Henry, the well-known Spartanburg lawyer, and Joel Smith, a prospective stockholder from Abbeville. (Henry had published a pamphlet four years earlier against a proposed constitutional amendment that sought to make all members of a South Carolina corporation "jointly and severally" liable for debts and liabilities of the company. Such an amendment, he pointed out, would have driven investors from the state.) After considerable debate the House reversed the committee's unfavorable report by a vote of 84 to 32. In the Senate the opposition was less formidable, and the bill easily passed the crucial second reading with a majority of 34 to 9. [11]

The charter of the Graniteville Manufacturing Company authorized it to operate for fourteen years on a capital investment of $300,000 in shares of $500 each, but it was necessary that $150,000 actually be paid in before the start of operations. Five years later the company had the charter extended for thirty years with the privilege of increasing its capital stock to $1,000,000. That year the company increased its capitalization to $360,000, at which amount it remained until after 1860.[12]

The Graniteville stockholders held a preliminary meeting in Horse Creek Valley in January, 1846, and two months later formally organized their company. They selected William

[11] *Journal of the House of Representatives of the State of South Carolina. Being the Annual Session of 1845* (Columbia, S.C., 1845), 102–103; *Journal of the Senate of the State of South Carolina. Being the Annual Session of 1845* (Columbia, S.C., 1845), 87; *Speech of Maj. James Edward Henry, on Productive Corporations*, 3–4, 11–14. A brief report of the debate appeared in the *Spartan* (Spartanburg), December 27, 1845.
[12] Graniteville Stockholders' Minutes (MS in Gregg Foundation Files, Graniteville Company, Graniteville, S.C.). In recent years the word "Manufacturing" has been dropped from the company's title.

Gregg as president, A. R. Taft treasurer, and General James Jones secretary. Jones, Taft, Hiram Hutchison, and C. K. Huger were chosen as directors. There was stability in the directorship, for during the next five years only one change occurred in the board—in 1848 James H. Taylor replaced Huger.[13]

From its inception the Graniteville company attracted a sufficient number of investors to carry out its program. Gregg later stated that he would not have undertaken its control had not enough capital been first subscribed to build the factory and to equip it completely. According to the plans of the original incorporators, a down payment of 5 percent of each subscription would be required at the first meeting, 5 percent in the fall of 1846, and the balance in 1847. However, although pledged, the entire capital was not collected until 1849. This was undoubtedly the reason that Gregg had to borrow large sums of money while the company was becoming established.[14]

Of the first thirty-two stockholders, there were twenty Charlestonians who held over 50 percent of the capital. Within three years the value of the stock had risen above par, and Gregg secretly but unsuccessfully tried to buy an additional $12,000 worth, at a premium, from another stockholder. Some trading did take place among other investors, with four selling out and three new ones buying in. The stockholders with the largest holdings were Ker Boyce, Joel Smith, and Hiram Hutchison, each with eighty shares; Gregg, with sixty shares, ranked fourth. Boyce, a Charleston factor, banker, and sometime state senator, exhibited shrewd business acumen, and almost every enterprise he touched proved successful. At the time of his death in 1854 he was one of the wealthiest men in South Carolina. Smith, of Abbeville District, was a planter, capitalist, and state legislator.

[13] Ibid.; Charleston Courier, January 6, March 13, 1846; Wallace, "A Hundred Years of William Gregg and Graniteville," 32–33.
[14] De Bow's Review, VI (October and November, 1848), 371; Charleston Courier, January 6, 1846, December 6, 1849; Speech of William Gregg, Member from Edgefield District in the Legislature of South Carolina, Dec., 1857, on the Bank Question (Columbia, S.C., 1857), 21.

At one time he owned stock in seventeen companies. Hutchison was a banker from Hamburg, South Carolina.[15]

After the formal organization of the Graniteville Manufacturing Company in March, 1846, the directors, for $11,000, purchased 7,952 acres of Horse Creek land and immediately began operations. About forty hands were put to work digging the canal, building the dams, and setting up the sawmill. Gregg acted both as administrator and engineer. His chief assistant was the highly-regarded Julius Petsch, who had been foreman of a Charleston iron foundry.[16] Gregg later explained his failure to engage a full-time engineer: "Having made manufacturing a study from 1837 to 1845, I felt that I was fully competent to the task of rearing this work without the aid of manufacturing engineers . . . whose undivided services would be obtained at a high cost and who might prove to be impracticable, wasteful, or possibly worse, speculative, aiming solely to make money on their account, out of us." [17]

In May, Gregg advertised for masons and carpenters to build the factory. He was his own designer and probably drew his ideas from some of the New England mills that he had seen. His plans called for a two-story building, 350 by 50 feet, with a high-roofed attic, and two front towers which enclosed staircases. Such a building would not require as expensive a foundation as would a taller one, nor would there be the problem of vibrations often found in higher walls. Also, the difficulty of elevating machinery and materials into the factory would be greatly lessened. The directors decided to construct the mill of locally quarried granite; and under the guidance of a Colonel Timanns the foundation was completed by October. At the same time the

[15] Gregg to James H. Hammond, May 30, 1849 (Photostatic copy in Gregg Foundation Files); Wallace, "Gregg and Graniteville," 20–33. In a period of about thirty years after Boyce's death, his heirs realized over $2,300,000 from his estate. See Account Book of the Division of the Estate of Ker Boyce (Manuscripts Division, Library of Congress).

[16] Mitchell, *William Gregg*, 40; Charleston *Courier*, March 13, 1846, March 24, 1848.

[17] Mitchell, *William Gregg*, 43–44, citing Gregg's report to stockholders, April 18, 1867.

sawmill was running full speed to supply lumber for the factory, the hotel, the warehouses, and the workers' homes. Other machines were busy making sashes, doors, and blinds.[18]

The power for the mill was supplied by two turbines, one at each end of the factory, while an additional engine at the sawmill was used as an auxiliary when needed. The granite dam normally created an ample supply of water, which was conducted by a canal to the mill three-fourths of a mile away. Upon reaching the factory, the water was relayed through two round pipes to the turbines, each capable of generating 116 horsepower.[19]

Some modern features of the Graniteville mill included a specially designed clock that required the watchman to visit each room at specific intervals. A series of small steam pipes furnished heat for the factory, while a number of four-inch water pipes gave fire protection. The steam came from an outside furnace, and the water pipes were constantly kept full by a force pump operating from one of the turbines. For drinking water the operatives depended on another pump, which kept a continuous flow coming up from a spring beneath the plant. Later the proprietors installed gas lighting in the main factory. With these innovations Graniteville was more up to date than many of its New England counterparts.[20]

In March, 1849, Gregg informed the stockholders that 9,245 spindles would be ready to operate June 1 and 300 looms by July 1. This made Graniteville by far the largest mill in antebellum South Carolina, if not in the entire South. According to Gregg, the company's total expenditures had amounted to $300,004, and he expected the final costs not to vary over $3,500 from that figure. The chief items were machinery, which had cost $122,000; factory buildings, $54,000; and dwelling houses,

[18] Charleston *Courier*, March 23–24, 1848; Wallace, "Gregg and Graniteville," 47; Mitchell, *William Gregg*, 44.
[19] Wallace, "Gregg and Graniteville," 38a. The canal was forty feet wide and six feet deep; the relay pipes were five feet in diameter and three hundred feet long. Charleston *Courier*, September 8, 1849.
[20] Charleston *Courier*, September 8, 1849.

$43,000. He boasted that the entire establishment had cost $32.44 per spindle compared with $35 to $38 per spindle in Lowell, Massachusetts. The spindles had been purchased from William Mason and Company, Taunton, Massachusetts, and much of the shafting and gearing had come from several Charleston foundries.[21]

A visitor in 1848 wrote of the impression that Graniteville's appearance first made upon him: "When Graniteville burst upon our view from the summit of the hill, its main building of white granite, 350 feet long, with two massive towers ornamented at the top, looking like some magnificent palace just rising out of the green vale below, with an extensive lawn in front, and clean trimmed, gravel walks around, and fountains spouting their crystal waters in the air in fantastic shapes. . . ." Along the canal were boarding houses, each with gardens and other conveniences, and built "with strict uniformity." On the hillsides rested the cottages for individual families. These dwellings, costing about $400 each, were constructed with peaked roofs, gothic windows, and ornamental eaves. To this picture another correspondent added that every cottage had its garden of flowers and vegetables. He was informed that the company had set out 10,000 rose cuttings, in addition to elm, water oak, and walnut trees, evergreens and grass plots. The yard at the factory was laid out with neatly-graded walks and lined with shrubbery. Gregg himself wrote that the village, comprising an area of 150 acres, contained two "handsome Gothic churches," an academy, a hotel, ten or twelve stores, and about a hundred cottages containing from three to nine rooms each.[22]

As the factory neared completion Gregg advertised for four hundred young female workers, preferably over fourteen years old, and thirty matrons. He had separate dwellings for families

[21] Wallace, "Gregg and Graniteville," 38a–39; Stockholders' Accounts, Graniteville Manufacturing Company (MS in South Caroliniana Library).
[22] De Bow's Review, VI (October and November, 1848), 370–71; Charleston Courier, September 7, 1849; Gregg to Freeman Hunt, October 22, 1849, in Hunt's Merchant's Magazine, XXI (December, 1849), 671–72.

that could furnish as many as four workers. The notice spoke highly of the churches, school, comfortable houses, and the good morals of the community. More subtle propaganda was employed in "A Voice From Graniteville," which advised the poor seamstresses to cease plying their needle for 12½ cents per garment. The "Voice" urged them instead of suffering in "silent poverty" to go to the Graniteville mill, whose president was a gentleman and whose superintendent would constantly look after their welfare and comfort. Their labor would be easy and each girl would have a window next to her loom, shaded by a curtain, where she could cultivate her potted flowers on the sill and "enjoy pure mountain air." [23]

Gregg soon learned that his proposed system of boardinghouses did not appeal to the girls, who were unwilling to leave their homes, but that the individual houses for families attracted large numbers. Here the mothers could perform the housework and the fathers could do the chores around the house and garden while the children worked in the factory. By October, 1849, the company had employed about 325 workers, who supported a village population of 900 whites. With the exception of the superintendent, the overseers, and several mechanics, nearly all were recruited from within twenty or thirty miles of Graniteville. The superintendent, James Montgomery, was from Scotland, and the four overseers were from Rhode Island.[24]

The hours of work began as soon as there was sufficient light to run the machines. Everyone had to be in attendance at the ringing of the second bell in the morning. The instant it ceased to ring the gates were locked, and all tardy workers were required to pass through the office. At 7 A.M. the mill shut down for forty-five minutes to allow the hands to eat breakfast, and at 1 P.M. there was a forty-five minute lunch period. Work con-

[23] Laurensville *Herald*, April 14, 1848; Charleston *Courier*, April 18, 1848.
[24] J. H. Taylor, "Manufactures in South Carolina," *De Bow's Review*, VIII (January, 1850), 28; *Hunt's Merchant's Magazine*, XXI (December, 1849), 671–72; Charleston *Courier*, September 8, 1849; Seventh U.S. Census, Free Inhabitants, South Carolina; Edgefield District (MS in National Archives).

tinued until 7:30 P.M. During the last hour and a half the plant usually depended upon artificial light. Twelve hours was the average work day. For their labor the male workers earned $4.00 to $5.00 per week, the females $3.00 to $4.00, and the children $1.00 to $2.00. Board was $1.50 per week. Gregg estimated these wages to be 20 percent lower than those of similar workers in Massachusetts.[25]

Graniteville began to ship shirting and sheeting to New York in May, 1849, and by July the mill, in full operation, was daily producing twelve hundred yards of shirting, sheeting, and drills of number 14 yarn. The merchants of Charleston, Philadelphia, and New York, said Gregg, quickly judged Graniteville cloth to be equal in quality to any of similar grade made elsewhere. When some of the Graniteville goods won first prize at an exhibition of the Franklin Institute in Philadelphia, newspapers in that city took favorable notice of the products for their neatness and "honest strength." They incorrectly predicted that South Carolina would soon become a tariff state.[26]

[25] Taylor, "Manufactures in South Carolina," 27–28; *Hunt's Merchant's Magazine*, XXI (December, 1849), 671–72; *The Plough, the Loom, and the Anvil*, II (July, 1849), 200.
[26] Wallace, "Gregg and Graniteville," 40; Charleston *Mercury*, November 5–6, 1849.

Chapter 5 Expansion, Contraction, & Reorganization

At the same time William Gregg and his associates were promoting Graniteville, there was considerable agitation for a cotton mill to be located in Charleston. Two such companies were chartered in the same month as Graniteville. One, the Ashley Manufacturing Company, was empowered to raise $200,000 for the purpose of manufacturing, bleaching, dyeing, and finishing textile fabrics. The other, the Belvidere Manufacturing Company, was authorized to raise a capital of $50,000. A news report several months later stated that some of the Ashley stock had been subscribed, but that the Belvidere stock had yet to be placed on the market. At least one would-be Ashley stockholder, Robert Martin, turned instead to Graniteville and possibly others did also. The Belvidere promoters may have been discouraged by the failure of their charter to grant the stockholders limited liability. In any case, neither company ever started operations.[1]

The interest in Charleston continued, nevertheless, and in May, 1847, a group of entrepreneurs organized the Charleston Cotton Manufacturing Company with James Chapman as president and James T. Welsman, Joseph Prevost, Henry Cobia, and James H. Taylor directors. Taylor was later credited with being the chief organizer behind the company, to which praise he modestly replied that the company's start was the result of well directed efforts of "several enterprising men." Shortly after their formal organization the directors called for a 5 percent installment to be paid on the stock, and in September they purchased a factory site in the Charleston suburb of Hampstead.[2]

[1] Charleston *Courier*, January 15, 1847, October 25, 1849; Edgefield *Advertiser*, April 1, 1849. In 1850 another abortive attempt was made when the Hayne Cotton Mill was chartered. Its members included two Graniteville stockholders.

[2] Charleston *Courier*, May 12, June 3, 1847, March 8–9, April 13, 1848; Charleston Deeds, Z–11, 530–32.

63

The company laid the cornerstone of its factory building on October 2 in an impressive ceremony reminiscent of that held by the South Carolina Homespun Company thirty-nine years earlier. James H. Taylor, in the absence of Chapman, delivered an oration to a large audience of townspeople. Afterwards Henry Cobia deposited a case in the cornerstone containing a list of stockholders, the newspapers of the day, Gregg's *Essays on Domestic Industry*, a coin of the United States, a cottonseed, and other articles.[3] A few weeks later the South Carolina General Assembly granted the company a charter of incorporation with its stock listed at $100,000 and with the privilege of increasing it to $500,000.

Once the cornerstone was laid, Walker and Saunders, construction engineers, hastened to complete the brick factory. It was three stories high and 196 by 50 feet in dimension. The company contracted with General Charles T. James of Rhode Island to furnish the machinery. James was already noted for his mills in the North, having by that time reputedly put up one-eighth of the spindles in the United States. The machinery, including a 60- to 70-horsepower steam engine, arrived in Charleston the latter part of March. With it came George Copeland, James's representative, to supervise the installation. When put into operation the factory contained 3,165 spindles and 100 looms, ranking it third in the state for size. The following year the company introduced gas lighting into the mill, a novelty which caused quite a sensation and drew a large crowd of curious spectators to witness its first use.[4]

In less than a year after laying the factory cornerstone the Charleston Cotton Manufacturing Company was advertising heavy shirting and sheeting, brown and bleached goods, and prints for sale. These goods, just as those of Graniteville, quickly received favorable notice from merchants and newspapers. They soon won first-class premiums at the fairs of the State Agricul-

[3] Charleston *Courier*, October 4, 1847.
[4] *Ibid.*, March 28, April 13, 1848, November 6, 1849; *Hunt's Merchant's Magazine*, XX (January, 1849), 115, XXII (April, 1850), 456–57.

tural Society, the South Carolina Institute, and Philadelphia's Franklin Institute. In 1849 the factory turned out 1,640,000 yards of cloth valued at $114,000. James H. Taylor, agent for the company, wrote Senator John C. Calhoun: "We regard our experiment as setling the question in relation to Manufacturing Cotton into Cloth to advantage by *steam*, in our Southern Cities, and I have the strongest hope that in a few years the manufacture of our own great staple will add to the Southern States incalculable wealth and prosperity." [5] It should be noted that the Charleston mill was the only cotton factory in antebellum South Carolina to use steam power to propel its machinery.

The company recruited its labor force mainly from the white boys and girls of Charleston. For those whose parents did not live near the cotton mill it offered boarding facilities. Nevertheless, it encountered considerable prejudice on the part of local citizens against the "degrading" work of a factory, and many seamstresses preferred to work for a pittance at home rather than enter a cotton mill. Taylor stated that this opposition was sufficient to hamper the operations of the plant. In addition to almost a hundred local hands, the company hired seventeen experienced Northern workers. [6]

The Charleston factory labored under the handicap of having too few spindles for the overhead expenses involved. William Gregg had previously warned against such a mistake, and Taylor soon recognized it to be a serious fault. He came to believe that the overhead costs were almost as much for a small mill of three thousand spindles as they were for one of twelve thousand. With this situation in mind the stockholders resolved to increase the capital stock to $500,000. To help them reach their goal General James made a very tempting offer: he would subscribe $200,000 provided the company obtained another $200,000. Amid opti-

<hr />

[5] Edgefield *Advertiser*, September 20, 1848; Charleston *Mercury*, May 14, 1850; Taylor to Calhoun October 3, 1848, in John C. Calhoun Papers; Seventh Census, Products of Industry, South Carolina: Charleston District.

[6] Taylor to Calhoun, October 3, 1848, in John C. Calhoun Papers; Taylor, "Manufactures in South Carolina," 29; Charleston *Courier*, February 18, 1848.

mistic reports by local newspapers the corporation opened its books, July 2–3, 1850, to welcome additional capital. On the first day one anonymous Charleston planter alone subscribed $50,000, and other investors raised the total to $100,000, but the company failed to realize the remainder of the amount necessary to take advantage of James's offer. In January the firm again opened its books, the balance having been reduced to $50,000, but its efforts proved unavailing. The Rhode Island promoter withdrew his offer shortly thereafter.[7]

Besides the Graniteville and Charleston mills several smaller factories were built during the years 1844 –50. The first of these was established by Dr. James Bivings, who had left Bivingsville because of an "unfounded jealousy" toward him on the part of some of the stockholders. He purchased a large tract of land on Chinquepin Creek just north of Spartanburg Court House and there began operations anew. He wrote on November 24, 1844: "I have my factory house up & if not prevented by bad weather I hope to have it covered & closed in, in two weeks." Although the mill contained only 264 spindles the proprietor discovered that his water power was too weak to propel the machinery. To supplement it he hitched mules to a long sweep attached to a revolving wheel. But this measure also proved ineffectual, and Bivings quickly decided to abandon Chinquepin.

In February, 1846, he informed his friend William Anderson that he had paid $2,000 for 650 acres of land, including a "beautiful shoal" on the Middle Tyger River and expected to begin work there within a week. With the aid of his son James D., he set up his buildings and equipped the mill with the machinery from his Chinquepin plant. He named the community Crawfordsville in honor of John Crawford, a nearby resident.

The next year a visitor to Crawfordsville glowingly reported that the machinery was of the most approved kind, turning off 50 percent more yarn per spindle than "any mill in the country." He pictured the factory building as "large and convenient," the workers' cabins "neat and well built," and the workers

[7] Gregg, *Domestic Industry*, 50–53; Taylor, "Manufactures in South Carolina," 29; Charleston *Courier*, July 2–3, 1850, January 23, 1851.

themselves possessing "countenances of contentment." Sometime during the 1850's Dr. Bivings expanded his plant and installed looms.[8]

Shortly after Bivings went to Crawfordsville, Gabriel Cannon, Joseph Finger, and Henry Kestler organized the Pacolet Manufacturing Company to produce yarn at Fingerville. Some years earlier Finger had migrated from North Carolina to upper Spartanburg District. According to tradition, he crossed the Pacolet with his wife on his back, spent the night in a cabin nearby, and decided to settle there. In 1840 he purchased a tract of land at McMillin's Shoals and put up a gristmill and some wool cards. Cannon, a public-spirited businessman who later became lieutenant governor of South Carolina, owned a large mercantile store at New Prospect, only two miles away.[9]

In their articles of partnership, drawn up February 1, 1848, the three men agreed to construct a mill which was not to exceed $10,000 in cost, all expenses to be borne equally. Kestler was to be in charge of erecting the buildings and fitting out the machinery, and afterwards to act as chief machinist for the concern. Cannon was to be the superintendent, bookkeeper, and selling agent. Finger was to be employed as a workman "and justly compensated." Within a year's time the partners had the factory in full operation. In 1860 it housed 396 spindles and employed thirteen hands.[10]

In 1850 J. Starke Sims opened a small yarn manufacturing and

---

[8] Landrum, *History of Spartanburg County*, 163; James Bivings to William Anderson, November 24, 1844, February 14, 1846, in William Anderson Papers, in possession of William D. Anderson, Gastonia, N.C.; Spartanburg Deeds, Z, 303–304, 306–307. A history of Bivings' activities and a description of Crawfordsville were published in the Charleston *Courier*, October 22, 1847. Employing only eleven hands, Bivings' small factory produced $10,500 worth of yarn in 1849. Ten years later the plant employed twenty-six workers and produced $4,820 worth of yarn and $11,520 worth of cloth. Seventh and Eight Censuses, Products of Industry, South Carolina: Spartanburg District.

[9] Spartanburg Deeds, X, 366–67. A sketch of Cannon's life is in Landrum, *Spartanburg County*, 437–39.

[10] Articles of partnership are in Spartanburg deeds, AA, 510–13. See also Eighth Census, Products of Industry, South Carolina: Spartanburg District.

wool carding mill at Grindal Shoals on the Pacolet River in Union District. This establishment, having only two hundred spindles in 1860, could claim the distinction of being the only cotton mill in antebellum Union District.[11]

Another small upcountry factory built during the 1840's was Daniel McCullough's yarn mill at Mount Dearborn on the Catawba River in lower Chester District. McCullough, a prominent Fairfield District planter, acted as his own architect, engineer, and overseer. With the aid of slave labor and a portable horse sawmill he built a wooden factory sufficient in size to house six hundred spindles. Later an editorial praised his yarn and called McCullough a man of "clear judgement, intelligent and industrious, and of ample means . . . [and] a gentleman of the right stamp for an enterprise of this kind." [12]

Meanwhile, in central South Carolina, the Laurel Falls factory was begun in February, 1848, near Lexington Court House. In December the legislature incorporated the Laurel Falls Manufacturing Company with Henry A. Meetze as president. John Caldwell, who was one of the seven other stockholders, seemed to be the chief financier. The factory, equipped with five hundred spindles and sixteen looms and employing twenty-two hands, began operations in January, 1849. Its machinery was powered by water from Twelve Mile Creek.[13]

As these various mills were being built, a movement got under way in Charleston to support the promotional work that Gregg and others had initiated earlier. General Abbott H. Brisbane, a former railroad builder and then currently a professor at the South Carolina Military Academy, approached former Gov-

[11] Eighth Census, Products of Industry, South Carolina: Union District; Rev. J. D. Bailey, *History of Grindal Shoals and Some Early Adjacent Families* (Gaffney, S. C., 1927), 21.

[12] *Southern Chronicle* (Columbia), April 30, 1845; *Daily Telegraph* (Columbia), October 21, 1847. McCullough may have equipped the factory at first with 600 spindles, but in 1860 it contained only 264 and appeared to be operating but part time. Eighth Census, Products of Industry, South Carolina: Chester District.

[13] *Daily Telegraph* (Columbia), March 10, 1849; Lexington Deeds, P, 668-69.

ernor James H. Hammond to lead the movement. But Hammond was apparently miffed that Brisbane considered him a retired statesman. Moreover, he expressed reluctance "to meddle with bubbles" and lay himself open to criticism, and so refused to head the proposed organization. Brisbane persisted, however, and secured the support of Gregg and other prominent businessmen. Hence, in early 1849 the South Carolina Institute was founded to promote "arts, mechanical ingenuity and industry." Gregg became its first president, while Brisbane strangely faded from the picture.[14]

In November of that year the South Carolina Institute, now counting several hundred members, held its first annual fair. Many types of handicraft and industrial products from South Carolina and neighboring states were exhibited amid glowing tributes from the local press. In addition, Hammond was persuaded by Gregg to deliver the main address. Ably supported by statistical information undoubtedly supplied by Gregg, Hammond discussed the economic benefits to be derived from the introduction of industry in the state. South Carolina had 35,000 poor whites eager to work in textile mills, Hammond said; they would work for longer hours and cheaper wages than English or Northern laborers. South Carolina's $7 million cotton crop, when processed, would bring $34 million. Furthermore, Hammond doubted that industrialization would undermine the South's attachment to free trade or slavery. He bluntly stated that it was time for the South to lay aside prejudices against manufacturing if the region wished to become prosperous.[15]

The institute held its second fair in November, 1850, this time with Judge Joseph H. Lumpkin of Georgia as the principal speaker. He followed the same line as had Hammond concerning the advantages of manufacturing but added unrealistically

---

[14] James H. Hammond to W. G. Simms, December 1, 1848 (Photostatic copy in Gregg Foundation Files); Wallace, "Gregg and Graniteville," 100–105; Charleston *Daily Courier*, November 22, 1856.

[15] *De Bow's Review*, VIII (June, 1850), 501–22; Charleston *Courier*, November 22, 1849.

that the southeastern states were "pushing ahead with giant strides." Even more amazingly, he said he knew of no bankruptcy of any cotton mill in the South.

The Charleston *Courier's* report of the third annual fair, November 17–26, 1851, made no mention of a speaker, but Gregg himself seems to have addressed the South Carolina Institute. The following month the institute secured a charter of incorporation from the legislature. At the next fair Edmund Ruffin, the prominent agricultural editor and scientist from Virginia, delivered the principal address, mainly a discussion of scientific agriculture and its benefits.[16]

The directors of the institute now decided to erect a large hall. The legislature, upon the recommendation of Governor John H. Means, appropriated $10,000 for that purpose; the Charleston City Council gave an additional $10,000 and loaned $25,000 more. The directors also received some private contributions. For reasons unknown the institute hall was slow to be erected and was not ready for use until late 1854. No fair was held in the interim, but on April 11, 1855, the South Carolina Institute opened its fifth fair amid the greatest fanfare it had ever attempted. For three months previously the institute advertised extensively, and even ran a two-column front-page ad in the *Daily Courier* for several days prior to the event. The South Carolina Railroad announced special rates for travelers to the fair; and during the two weeks that the fair was open the *Daily Courier* carried lengthy items about it, including front-page coverage of Congressman James L. Orr's address.[17]

The 1855 and 1856 fairs marked a turning point in the institute's history. Later fairs were held, but the variety of exhibits

[16] J. H. Lumpkin, "Industrial Regeneration of the South," *De Bow's Review*, XII (January, 1852), 41–50; Charleston *Daily Courier*, November 19, 1852; William Gregg, "Manufactures in South Carolina and the South," *De Bow's Review*, XI (August, 1851), 123–40. On July 1, 1852, the *Courier* became the *Daily Courier*.

[17] Charleston *Daily Courier*, November 24, 1852, April 9–30, 1855, November 22, 1856.

declined and interest waned. It was all too obvious by the late fifties that neither flowery oratory, optimistic statistical data, newspaper fanfare, nor appeals to Southern patriotism could induce South Carolina entrepreneurs to invest more than modest sums in industry.

The dismal results were clearly revealed by the history of South Carolina textiles in the 1850's, during which decade only one new cotton mill was built. It was erected on Lawson's Fork at Valley Falls in 1857 by the veteran manufacturer John Weaver in partnership with William D. McMakin. Weaver retained his interest in the plant but a short time, selling out to his partner the following year and returning to Greenville District.[18]

As a matter of fact, even before the expansion movement in textiles had reached its peak in about 1849, its contraction was already under way. John E. Colhoun's mill at Pendleton ceased operations in the early forties; on November 10, 1848, fire destroyed Jeptha Dyson's Fulton factory with a loss of $30,000;[19] and, as has been seen, Dr. Bivings' Chinquepin factory was strictly a temporary affair.

The next mill to cease operations was the Marlboro factory, built in 1838 by John N. Williams, John McQueen, and William T. Ellerbe. About 1840 Meekin Townsend acquired part interest in the factory, which was then making little or no profit. The other partners repeatedly, but unsuccessfully, sought a purchaser for their remaining interest. In 1847, after some of the machinery had been disposed of, Townsend liquidated his partners' remaining holdings. His sole proprietorship was short lived, for on December 31, 1850, a spectacular fire destroyed the factory. So rapid was the spread of flames through the building

18 *Southern Enterprise* (Greenville), January 22, 1857, August 25, 1858; Spartanburg Deeds, FF, 352-53. In 1860 the factory housed 420 spindles and employed 14 workers. Eighth Census, Products of Industry, South Carolina: Spartanburg District.

19 *Daily Telegraph* (Columbia), November 17, 1848. This writer found no reference to Colhoun's plant after 1840. In 1849 Colhoun's widow advertised his estate for sale. See *Keowee Courier* (Pickens), October 13, 1849.

that some workers had to leap from second-story windows to escape. A news item placed the loss at $22,000. [20]

At Lexington the recently-established Laurel Falls cotton mill burned in February, 1852; while only three months later the Charleston Cotton Manufacturing Company folded. Having failed to secure $200,000 in additional capital to match General James's offer, the stockholders sold their property at auction in May. The machinery was dismantled and shipped away.[21]

The next to go was the DeKalb factory, built at Camden in 1838 and incorporated in 1846 as the DeKalb Manufacturing Company with the privilege of raising $150,000 capital. The chief stockholders were Thomas J. Ancrum, A. Young, William Gardner, the superintendent, and the original founders, William Anderson, Burwell Boykin, and Thomas Lang. The chartered company increased the spindles from 1,000 to 1,680 and the working force from 50 to 94.

After enjoying several seemingly prosperous years, the stockholders became dissatisfied with the progress of the company. They advertised the mill for sale but had found no purchaser before a fire in December, 1855, totally destroyed the building and its contents. It was the most costly cotton mill fire in antebellum South Carolina history: the loss was estimated at between $40,000 and $50,000. [22]

None of the factories listed which burned was ever rebuilt. It may have been due to the fact that none was adequately protected by insurance. Laurel Falls, with $7,000 insurance on $10,000 worth of property, had the best coverage of any. In addition to these and the Charleston mill, John N. Williams' plant at Society Hill ceased operations sometime before 1860, leaving not a single cotton factory below the fall line.

[20] Charleston *Courier*, March 24, 1842, October 8, 1845, January 3, 1851; Marlboro Deeds, R, 358, Q, 150–52.

[21] Charleston *Courier*, February 27, May 5, 1852. The Graniteville Manufacturing Company unsuccessfully attempted to exchange a new issue of Graniteville stock for the Charleston machinery. See Graniteville Stockholders' Minutes, July 14, 1852.

[22] Camden *Journal*, June 30, 1849, January 26, 1852, December 18, 1855.

Besides the demise of these eight textile mills in the two decades preceding the Civil War, several others underwent changes of ownership and reorganization. One of these was the Bivingsville Manufacturing Company. Two years after Dr. James Bivings left to free-lance on his own, George and Elias C. Leitner bought the controlling share of the company's stock. Of their transactions A. W. Bivings made a dire prognostication: "Father has sold his stock to E. C. Leitner & Brother for $13600 and taken their notes with mortgage. They have purchased Forty nine thousand Dollars of the original Stock & I prophesy that it will wind them up in the ten Years of time Embraced as a credit." [23]

In 1850 an editor in nearby Greenville published some alarming financial statistics concerning the Bivingsville company. The expenses were disclosed at $33,680 against $32,000 as the value of its products. But the Spartanburg newspaper immediately took issue: "If the Southern Patriot is correct in its findings of our 'greatness' our friend Col. Leitner had better stop operations of that large and beautiful establishment at Bivingsville. What say you, Col. Leitner?" [24]

Elias C. Leitner issued no public statement. Ironically enough, A. W. Bivings and the Greenville editor had correctly forecast his financial debacle. The "Colonel" shortly burned his books and disappeared, never to be heard from again. In March, 1856, during bankruptcy proceedings, the establishment was sold for $19,500, less than one-third of the original capitalized value.[25] The purchaser was the John Bomar and Company, composed of John Bomar, Jr., Vardry McBee, Simpson Bobo, John C.

[23] Bivings to William Anderson, February 11, 1846, in William Anderson Papers. The Leitners' finances became very tangled. Besides their debt to Dr. Bivings, they owed $34,500 to nine other people, mainly former stockholders of the company. Spartanburg Deeds, Z, 242–45, 289–91, 295–98, 314, 332–33, 424–25.

[24] *Spartan* (Spartanburg), March 27, 1851.

[25] Yorkville *Enquirer*, March 27, 1856. Leitner is believed to have fled to Texas. Some years later an anonymous envelope containing a picture resembling him was sent to John E. Bomar in Spartanburg. Interview with Mr. Jesse Cleveland, Spartanburg, S.C., October 12, 1948.

Zimmerman, S. N. Evins, and Dexter C. Converse, all of whom
were experienced textile manufacturers. Bomar acted as manager
and Converse, a newcomer from the mills of New York, was
named superintendent. The stockholders immediately took measures to put the idle
factory back into working order. At the same time they laid
down definite rules designed to govern the financial operations
not only of the mill but of the farm, boarding house, store, and
machine shop as well. The manager was instructed to run the
establishment with "utmost caution & prudence." Their policy
proved to be quite effective, for the company soon thereafter
showed signs of returning prosperity. By the end of the decade
their buildings and improvements were valued at $26,000; all
stock subscriptions had been paid; all notes had been met on
time; and the treasury showed a surplus of over $8,000. [26]

Vaucluse, which had experienced a turbulent history in the
1830's, changed hands several times during the next two decades.
John Bauskett, its sole owner in 1840, found its management
too confining to allow adequate time for his other activities. The
next year he therefore sold half ownership to General James
Jones on the condition that Jones would manage the factory.
Two years later Bauskett retired altogether, relinquishing his
remaining share to William Gregg, who, in partnership with
his brother-in-law Jones, operated Vaucluse for five years.[27]

Both proprietors had studied cotton manufacturing in the
North, and they decided to renovate the plant. They repaired,
changed, and increased the machinery until the mill was operating 2,280 spindles and 43 looms. They concentrated their pro-

[26] Stockbook, J. Bomar & Co. (MS in possession of Glendale Mill, Glendale, S.C.). In 1860 the mill was equipped with 1,435 spindles and 26 looms.
It employed 58 workers. Eighth Census, Products of Industry, South
Carolina: Spartanburg District. Bobo and Evins soon withdrew from the
company.

[27] John Bauskett to Thomas Bauskett, February 7, 1841, in Thomas Wadlington Papers (Photostatic copies in Duke University Library); Edgefield Deeds, CCC, 30–32, 473–74.

duction on osnaburgs, and the factory, so it was said, paid for itself in five years.[28]

After Gregg became engrossed in his duties at Graniteville, he sold his interest in Vaucluse to Jones and took a mortgage on the property to secure payment. For almost ten years Jones was sole proprietor of the concern; however, he failed to rid himself of his debt to Gregg. When he was appointed in 1856 to superintend the construction of the new statehouse, Jones sought to dispose of Vaucluse, but newspaper advertisements brought him no acceptable offer. As a last resort he turned to Gregg and entreated him to purchase it. Jones wrote: "I should not be solicitous to sell the property at the present time; but I cannot stand the interest upon your debt and the insurance on the property with the Mill standing idle. I must therefore either sell it or go back and run it. . . . I think the property dog cheap at $25000. and that you ought to take it at that price from me. But if you do not agree with me as to price, make me an offer and I will consider it. . . ." [29]

Gregg did not think that $25,000 was "dog cheap" for Vaucluse. A year later he drove a hard bargain with his brother-in-law and paid him only $16,500 for the entire property. He placed his son James in charge, and the two, under the name of J. J. Gregg and Company, outfitted the mill with several hundred new spindles, reconditioned the old ones, and eliminated the weaving department. The factory, after three years of idleness, resumed operations in June, 1859. [30]

The Saluda Company also went through the throes of reorganization several times. When the company, with Edward H. Fisher as its head, bought out the Saluda Manufacturing Company, it appeared as though the mill might at last begin to enjoy

[28] De Bow's Review, VIII (November, 1849), 457–58, XI (September, 1851), 543.

[29] James Jones to William Gregg, July 10, 1856, in possession of Gregg Foundation Files; Edgefield Deeds, EEE, 439–41, 628.

[30] Edgefield Deeds, KKK, 508; Letterbooks, J. J. Gregg & Co. (MSS in South Caroliniana Library), I, 175–81.

prosperity. But multifold difficulties soon discouraged the new stockholders, and in less than five years they were ready to sell out. No buyers stepped forward; consequently, they struggled on, sinking more than $100,000, exclusive of the cost of slaves, into the enterprise. In 1853, despairing of any ultimate success, they placed the Negroes on the block, and two years later they sold the factory and remaining property to Dr. Robert W. Gibbes, the company president, and his son James G. Gibbes for a mere $20,000. [31]

When James G. Gibbes and Company took control of the Saluda mill, it acquired a factory with 5,196 spindles and 120 looms, but this equipment had lain idle for some time and was in a poor state of repair. It took more than a year to renovate the machinery and get the factory back into operation. In the meantime, the company had to construct new houses for the incoming operatives and repair the dam, which had been badly damaged by a winter freshet.

The new company changed the name of the factory to Columbia Mills and secured as superintendent Gilbert Reed, a former overseer of the Charleston cotton mill. A local editor called him "a practical manufacturer of high character." The workers were recruited entirely from local whites. In the fall of 1856 Columbia Mills sent some osnaburgs and other goods to the fair held by the South Carolina Institute in Charleston. They elicited high praise from the *Daily Courier:* "The Columbia Factory, after several ineffectual spasmodic efforts, has at length got into good hands, and bids fair to contribute its share toward the good work of [manufacturing]." This favorable prediction was largely borne out during the next few years.

Columbia Mills at first mainly produced osnaburgs, but in 1857 or 1858 the proprietors installed $20,000 worth of ma-

---

[31] Lexington Deeds, U, 41–42. Advertisements of the factory for sale appeared in the *Southern Chronicle* (Columbia), August 28, 1844–January 15, 1845, Charleston *Daily Courier*, December 10, 1852, and the Columbia *Banner*, April 12, 1854. The company's slaves—about 100—sold for an average price of $599. Charleston *Daily Courier*, January 4, 1853.

chinery to manufacture woolen plains, kerseys, and jeans. On the eve of the Civil War the factory, with 250 workers and an annual production of $230,000 worth of goods, ranked second to Graniteville, whose yearly output was valued at $289,736. [32]

Besides the reorganization of Bivingsville, Vaucluse, and Saluda, some of the smaller establishments also changed ownership. The South Tyger factory at Cedar Hill passed through the hands of several proprietors. The six partners who had purchased it in 1840 from the Reverend Thomas Hutchings sold it less than a year later to David W. Moore and James McMakin. Moore became sole owner in 1845 and later leased, or sold, the factory to Peter M. Wallace, editor of the *Spartan*. Wallace's creditors forced him into bankruptcy in 1859, after which Samuel N. Morgan, a local merchant and farmer, secured control. The plant at that time operated eight hundred spindles.[33]

Thomas M. Cox joined William Bates in 1847 at Batesville. Two years later Henry Pinckney Hammett, Bates's son-in-law, also became a partner in what was then called William Bates and Company. This enterprise, with Bates as president and Hammett as business manager, prospered and increased its capital from $20,000 in 1850 to $50,000 in 1860. No other cotton factory in South Carolina showed such a proportionate increase in capital during the same decade. Bates's factory on the eve of the Civil War boasted of twelve hundred spindles, thirty-six looms, and seventy operators. Of the upcountry mills, only Bivingsville was larger.[34]

A mile away, on the Enoree, Philip C. Lester and Josiah Kilgore operated Thomas Hutchings' old factory from about 1830

[32] *Daily South Carolinian* (Columbia), April 12, 1856; Charleston *Daily Courier*, November 29, 1856, December 21, 1859; Eighth Census, Products of Industry, South Carolina: Lexington and Edgefield districts. A detailed description of the Saluda factory appeared in the Columbia *Banner*, February 15, 1853.

[33] Spartanburg Deeds, X, 323, 467–68, Z, 152; *Carolina Spartan* (Spartanburg), January 20, 1859; Eighth Census, Products of Industry, South Carolina: Spartanburg District.

[34] Greenville Deeds, U, 127, V, 396, W, 182; Seventh and Eighth Censuses, Products of Industry, South Carolina: Greenville District.

until a fire destroyed it in 1853. The partners had no insurance on the property, and suffered a loss of $12,000. Kilgore then sold his interest in the remaining property to Lester, who rebuilt the mill, installed about five hundred spindles, and took in his three sons as partners to operate the factory, to be known henceforth by the name of Lester and Sons.[35]

As for the remaining textile companies in South Carolina, apparently none underwent any changes in ownership sudden or radical enough to produce a complete shake-up of administration. It should be noted, however, that in several cases sons joined their fathers as part owners or managers. Alex McBee and James D. Bivings are two such examples. After Leonard Hill's death in 1840 his four sons jointly inherited his property, but two eventually surrendered their interests in the mill to their two other brothers, James and Albert. And at Graniteville the deaths of Joel Smith, Hiram Hutchison, and Ker Boyce, which all occurred between March 19, 1854, and April 23, 1857, removed the three largest stockholders. In 1859, J. J. Blackwood, with 108 shares, thus became the leading investor. The number of stockholders also increased, from thirty-one in 1849 to fifty-nine in 1859. At that time A. R. Taft was the only member of the original board of directors still serving in that capacity. The nearest that Graniteville came to a reorganization occurred in the same year when Gregg and some of the directors clashed over several operational policies. At a special meeting in Charleston, Gregg offered to resign, but the majority of the stockholders took a neutral attitude and smoothed out the differences between the president and the board.[36]

[35]Laurensville *Herald*, July 22, 1853; Greenville Deeds, Y, 278, 661–66. In 1860 there was a small factory with eight workers listed as property of S. H. Turperfield or Turbyfill. This may have been Hudson Berry's old factory. Eighth Census, Products of Industry, South Carolina: Greenville District.

[36] Alex McBee managed Vardry McBee's cotton mill during the forties and the fifties. See miscellaneous letters in William P. McBee Papers, South Caroliniana Library. An account of the Hills' is in Landrum, *Spartanburg County*, 157–61. In 1859 the other large shareholders of the Graniteville company were James P. Boyce, 100; estate of Joel Smith, 100; and Gregg, 79. Graniteville Stockholders' Minutes.

Table 2

Cotton Manufacturing 1840—Selected States

State	Factories	Spindles	Employees	Capital
Mass.	278	665,095	20,928	$17,414,099
R.I.	209	518,817	12,086	7,326,000
Va.	18	40,472	1,735	1,250,720
N.C.	25	31,700	1,219	995,300
Ga.	16	17,600	800	590,000
S.C.	16	16,300	570	500,000
Tenn.	30	16,813	800	463,240

Source: *Compendium of the Sixth Census*, 112, 160, 184, 196, 208, 256, with estimated corrections by author for obvious errors in returns from the five Southern states. Statistics on production are too unreliable for use.

Cotton Manufacturing 1860—Selected States

State	Factories	Spindles	Employees	Capital	Production
Mass.	217	1,673,498	38,451	$33,704,674	$ 38,004,255
N.H.	44	636,788	12,730	12,586,880	13,699,994
Ga.	33	85,186	2,813	2,126,103	2,371,207
Va.	16	49,440	1,441	1,367,543	1,489,971
Ala.	14	35,740	1,312	1,316,000	1,040,147
N.C.	39	41,884	1,764	1,272,750	1,046,047
Tenn.	30	29,850	899	965,000	698,122
S.C.	18	26,000	891	820,000	713,050
11 Southern States	159	290,359	9,906	$ 9,596,221	$ 8,145,067
United States	1,091	5,235,727	122,028	$98,585,269	$115,681,774

Source: *Manufactures of the United States in 1860; Compiled from the Original Returns of the Eighth Census, under the Direction of the Secretary of the Interior* (Washington, 1865), xxi, with estimated corrections in the returns from South Carolina. Published returns for 1860, in contrast to the returns for 1840, revealed few obvious errors.

A review of antebellum textile development in South Carolina indicates three main periods of activity: (1) 1807–14, (2) 1828–38, (3) 1845–50. South Carolina's peak year was 1849. There were twenty-one mills in operation in the state at that time. Thereafter the number was reduced by subsequent business failures. Most other Southern states followed a similar pattern in their textile development, and, excepting Alabama, they also suffered a decline in the fifties in number of firms in operation.[37] Between 1840 and 1860 there was, in South Carolina, an overall increase from sixteen factories, with $500,000 capital and 16,300 spindles, to eighteen factories, with $820,000 capital and 26,000 spindles. Graniteville alone, with $360,000 capital and 9,245 spindles, made up the difference.

Elsewhere, Massachusetts, with $17,414,000 capital and 665,-000 spindles in 1840 and $33,704,000 capital and 1,673,000 spindles in 1860, dwarfed the output of the entire South. Within the South itself, South Carolina's larger and more populous neighbors surpassed the Palmetto State. The leaders in 1840 were Virginia and North Carolina. During the forties Georgia forged ahead, and by 1860 it led with $2,126,000 capital and 85,000 spindles. Virginia ranked second with $1,387,000 capital and 49,000 spindles.[38]

[37] In North Carolina, Standard and Griffin found, five mills were attempted and one completed 1804–14, twenty-five built 1828–40, and twenty built 1845–50, yet the published census returns listed the North Carolina mills as twenty-five, twenty-eight, and thirty-nine for the years 1840, 1850, and 1860, respectively. See Standard and Griffin, "Cotton Textile Industry in Ante-Bellum N. C.," 33–35, 133, 150.

[38] See accompanying table on page 79. Insufficient attention has been given to the Georgia textile industry to explain the reasons for its primacy in the South in 1860.

Chapter 6 Personnel & Paternalism

The failure of the South Carolina antebellum textile industry to make greater progress can be readily under-
stood when one considers the conditions under which
the average entrepreneur worked and the many problems he
encountered. The first problem facing the textile manufacturer,
once his factory was built, was that of procuring trained personnel. At its inception the South Carolina industry depended
almost wholly on the North and Europe for overseers and machinists, and as late as 1860 a large number still came from outside the South. Quite naturally, however, more and more native
citizens gradually moved into the highly skilled jobs and managerial positions.[1]

Unfortunately, to the extent of their own undoing, the entrepreneurs through carelessness or ignorance often placed incom-
petent men in important supervisory posts. After having seen
a number of Southern mills make the grevious mistake of hiring
inexperienced managers, John Hagarty, a veteran English textile
worker, advised the Southerners to go to England to select their
overseers from among numerous applicants. He gave a brief re-
sumé of the complex subjects a good manager ought to know

[1] In 1850 of 19 superintendents, overseers, and machinists known to
have been connected with Graniteville and Vaucluse, 6 were born in the
British Isles and 8 in the North. At that time the Saluda overseers were reported to be mainly from the North. Of 285 workers identified as having
been with Vaucluse and Graniteville in 1860 only 2 were from the North,
while 18, mainly machinists, were from Europe. Of 55 workers identified
with Bates's and Lester's factories 2 overseers were born in the North; the
remainder were natives of North or South Carolina. At Bivingsville the
superintendent and one bookkeeper were from New York, and one other
worker was from Ireland. Seventh U.S. Census, Free Inhabitants, South
Carolina: Edgefield District; Eighth U.S. Census, Free Inhabitants, S.C.:
Edgefield, Greenville, and Spartanburg districts (MSS in National Archives); Charleston *Mercury*, August 15, 1850. It is impossible to identify
all the workers in a given factory, as census takers often failed to list
occupations.

and added that such information could be attained only through experience.[2]

William Gregg cited several cases of poor management. In 1837 he found an ignorant Englishman in charge of Vaucluse. "He knew nothing of the business, and as was afterwards proved, had never before had charge, even of a single department in a mill. He was, in fact, only a common operative, with neither truth nor honesty in him." Later, at Saluda, James G. and Robert W. Gibbes hired a superintendent whom Gregg described as a "Notionate fellow who could not be trusted to get new Machinery, or to make many alterations with the old." He warned the Gibbeses of their overseer's limitations, but they were "captivated with his skill & activity and soon began to yield to opportunities to have slight alterations made & some new machines purchased." Within three years the owners had spent $30,000 and "could scarcely see where the money had gone." They hired a new overseer.[3]

One example of the difficulties an owner encountered in getting capable overseers was exhibited at Vaucluse in 1859–61. James Gregg's arrangement called for overseers of the carding, spinning, and reeling departments with assistant overseers for each. The head carder was to be superintendent of the entire establishment. In order to fill these positions, he wrote to several applicants, to his selling agents in the North, and to companies from whom he purchased machinery and offered $1.50 to $2.00 a day for the various jobs. As it was, it took several months to hire the necessary men, and then Gregg was not satisfied with some of his choices. In August, 1859, he was thinking of changing his reeling overseer, and a few days later he was seek-

---

[2] Charleston *Courier*, February 19, 1845.

[3] Gregg, *Essays on Domestic Industry*, 34; Report of William Gregg to Graniteville stockholders, June 22, 1859, Graniteville Stockholders' Minutes (MS in Gregg Foundation Files, Graniteville Company, Graniteville, S.C.). The superintendent at Saluda to whom Gregg referred was doubtless Gilbert Reed, a former superintendent at Charleston and later employed by Vardry McBee in Greenville. See *Daily South Carolinian* (Columbia), April 12, 1856; *Keowee Courier* (Pickens), July 3, 1858.

ing a good carder. He wrote his father in October that he had a reeling overseer who he thought would soon learn, but that his spinner, a man named Shell, was confined to bed. Fortunately, Shell's substitute, Walker, was a more efficient supervisor. Gregg added that Shell, upon recovery, either would have to manage his department better or be replaced altogether.

Gregg promoted Walker to superintendent, although this arrangement was also short-lived because the latter in August, 1860, decided to leave Vaucluse and buy a farm. Gregg had several applications for the position but found it difficult to secure the sort of man he desired. However, he ultimately offered $2.50 a day to William Perry, an experienced New Jersey overseer then working in Greenville District. As late as March, 1861, Gregg was still looking for a "first rate carder." In the meantime, George Kelly, a former superintendent at Graniteville, had been hired to supervise Vaucluse, and James Gregg himself prepared to move over to Graniteville to take "general charge." [4]

In several instances fathers trained their sons to become superintendents or business managers. This proved to be a happy solution in many cases. Robert Gibbes, James Bivings, and Philip Lester successfully pursued such a policy, and William Bates showed wisdom in making his son-in-law Henry P. Hammett business manager of Batesville. But in at least one instance the father-son partnership did not turn out well: that between Vardry McBee and his son Alex. The elder McBee dealt too sternly with all his children and permitted them too little freedom of action, even after they were middle-aged. His stubbornness is revealed in two letters from Alex to his brother Pinckney in 1857. Vardry would not permit Alex to build a house near the mill in order to have his family close at hand. Instead, Alex had to make his quarters in one small room, and whenever he approached his father on the subject, he merely aroused the old man's anger. Alex complained: "Surely after doing a very disagreeable business almost night & day for *13 years* I *am* entitled

[4] Letterbooks, J. J. Gregg & Co. (MSS in South Caroliniana Library), I, 219, 236, 279, II, 295, 318, 323, 351–52, 478.

to *some* sort of house to *stay in.*" He further declared that his father did not believe his children could do anything.[5]

For his part Vardry McBee was far from pleased with his son's management of the cotton mill. A few weeks earlier he had confided to Pinckney: "Alex is in trouble now & I am low sperited [as] it is now divulged that the factory has been loosing money & I suppose a goodeal." The elder McBee said that Alex and Adams, an overseer, had permitted the stream to undermine the water-wheel. Their only thought was to try to keep the news from him. He remonstrated: ". . . but is it not to be denied that all my children can subtract but none can add & continue to take from a mountain & you will remove the whole at last." [6]

William Gregg ran into some problems of his own in the management of Graniteville, especially in the use of his sons there. Under his own guidance the company had prospered and expanded. After 1852 it paid regular dividends, 10 percent yearly from 1855 through 1857. In 1855 Gregg publicly declared that he would not attempt to build another mill such as Graniteville for $50,000 above the original costs. For example, many of the temporary wooden dams and spillways had since been replaced with permanent structures of brick or stone.[7] But the Panic of 1857 shook the financial foundations of Graniteville. Gregg himself was forced to lend the company $90,000 to prevent it from suspending operations, and he had to endorse the company's notes to purchase cotton in Augusta. Although the depression quickly passed, it left several grievances between the president and the board of directors which came to a head in a meeting held in April of 1859. Some of the board members viewed with alarm the continued infiltration of Gregg's four sons into positions of importance. In addition, they felt that he

[5] Alex McBee to Pinckney McBee, January 11, February 16, 1857, in William P. McBee Papers, South Caroliniana Library.

[6] Vardry McBee to Alex McBee, December 24, 1856, in Malinda P. Landrum Papers, in 1948 in possession of Mrs. T. J. Mauldin, Pickens, S.C., now deceased.

[7] Wallace, "A Hundred Years of William Gregg and Graniteville," 90; William Gregg, "Practical Results of Southern Manufactures," 777–79.

was neglecting his duties at Graniteville for the sake of politics and for the mill at Vaucluse, which was being re-equipped by him and his son James at that time. Two other issues of disagreement pertained to Graniteville's marketing policy and Gregg's loan to the company.

Gregg called the stockholders to a special meeting in Charleston on June 22, of that year. There, before twenty-one members representing almost 90 percent of the shares, he read a five-thousand-word report in defense of his management. It was the criticism of the employment of his sons that seemed to rankle him most, and against this charge he fired his heaviest salvos. Gregg stated that he had spoiled the company by laboring in its behalf for eight years without pay. The directors now wanted to pay his son William only $50 per month as treasurer; William, however, was not inclined to work for so small an amount. In order to retain his services, Gregg in 1858 had paid his son $1,000 out of his own salary of $2,500 as president but was unwilling to do so again. At the meeting in April, and again in May, the directors had failed to take any action on his proposal that $2,500 be paid the president and $2,000 be paid to a treasurer whom the board might name. His son resigned and Gregg, by letter, informed the board that he would take both positions for $5,000. He fully intended to hire his son, or someone else, to perform the treasurer's duties and pay him out of his own salary. The board doubted its right to take such action; whereupon, Gregg, having lost his patience, accused them of ignorance of the company's affairs.

Securing a treasurer had been of great concern to him, Gregg continued. James H. Taylor, the first to hold the position, refused to live at Graniteville for less than $3,000 per year, and the superintendent knew nothing of such matters. Consequently, Gregg had had to act as treasurer. When William Gregg, Jr., returned from college, the elder Gregg had him undergo a thorough apprenticeship in a mercantile house and in both the outside department and the office at Graniteville. "He more than realized my expectations as a financier and business man and bid fair to be able at no distant day to manage your mercantile and general business more ably than I have ever been able to do," Gregg said. "Why gentlemen how could I come to the conclusion to permit matters to remain in the shape they were, as I considered myself under the imputation of having asked the board, for the services of my Son and myself, more than we were worth to the company. Rather than remain under such imputation, I would close the Factory, and abandon my interest in it."

As for his son James, Gregg stated that he had spent two years in the machine shop and factory, some months observing the textile industry in New England, and a year in Europe. He was at that time in charge of Vaucluse "in his own account," while a younger son was working in the Graniteville machine shop. Vigorously defending the employment of his sons, Gregg lashed out at the opposition: "Some stockholders have openly accused me of desiring to make sinecures for my sons at the expense of the G'ville company. There was never a more unjust accusation, ... for I have never allowed anyone to eat idle bread. I have impressed upon them that they should be examples to the workers around them and have instructed the overseers to treat them just as they do other employees." It was his policy, Gregg said, to interest his sons in the manufacture of cotton in order that the company might be able to acquire competent managers after he was gone.

Although Gregg devoted less attention to the other criticism, he did not allow it to remain unanswered. He quickly reminded the stockholders that his loan of $90,000 had benefited them more than it had him, for he easily could have secured from 12 to 20 percent interest on the money during the panic. He also denied that politics had taken up much of his time. In 1856 he had spent only four days campaigning for the House, and in 1858 he had agreed to run for the Senate on the belief that there would be no opposition. As it so happened, Tillman Watson came out against him, and then Gregg's friends would not hear of his withdrawal. He assured the stockholders he would become involved in no such hot campaign again.

Gregg denied that Vaucluse was in competition with Graniteville as some charged. Admitting that the building of a dam there had required some of his attention, he informed the company that in the future he would merely give James occasional advisory opinion regarding Vaucluse operations. With regard to the sales policy, he preferred to install the English system of selling at the factory. He was convinced it could be handled effectively in that manner with a saving of several thousand dollars in commissions.

Gregg concluded by boasting of Graniteville's success under his management. Its reputation was so widespread that a "shingle" stuck out anywhere "would attract the attention of everybody that passes" and bring unsought customers. Dramatically, he placed his cards on the table by saying, "Whenever you are tired of me Gentlemen I am ready to quit your service, there is no other Corporation in existence I would hire my time to. You may get a talented agent, but rest assured, if he be a lazy man he will permit your property to go to dilapidation. . . . If he be a visionary man he will waste your profit and capital in alterations & improvements that are not needed."

Acting favorably upon a committee report, the stockholders expressed "unbounded confidence" in Gregg and the board. They regretted the misunderstanding, expressed sorrow at losing the services of William Gregg, Jr., and hoped they might be secured again. They welcomed the reopening of Vaucluse and regarded it "as an additional security to our own interests at Graniteville." Gregg was appointed president and treasurer at $5,000 a year until a suitable man could be secured as treasurer.[8]

Gregg thus remained in firm control at Graniteville, and in 1860 his son William was elected to the board of directors. Nevertheless, the sales policy remained unchanged, and Gregg doubtless did not dispel from the stockholders' minds the fear of nepotism as they viewed the possible ultimate employment of all four of his sons.[9]

[8] Graniteville Stockholders' Minutes.
[9] Wallace, "Gregg and Graniteville," 141.

For machine operators, the central and lower South Carolina mills prior to 1840 depended mainly on slaves. Some factories used slaves exclusively except as overseers and superintendents, and David R. Williams was even reputed to have employed a Negro as superintendent of his Society Hill factory at one time. His son John N. Williams had used a highly skilled black mechanic to construct and install part of the machinery used at the mill. Meanwhile, nearly all upcountry mills used white labor exclusively.[10]

Generally, reports concerning the use of slaves in factories were favorable, but with the advent of the Graniteville, Charleston, and Laurel Falls factories in the 1840's a controversy arose over the relative merits of white and Negro labor. Apparently what caused the dispute was the fact that the three new factories relied on white workers alone.[11]

The protagonists for the use of slaves in the mills found a staunch champion in the *Daily Telegraph*, a Columbia newspaper. Its editor believed that white people, rather than working in cotton mills, could be more profitably and pleasantly employed "in other industrial pursuits requiring more intelligence and exacting less severe labor." In support of his theories he published a lengthy testimonial from one J. Graves, currently the superintendent of Saluda, which at that time employed about a hundred Negroes. Graves admitted that he had been prejudiced against slave workers when he first arrived from the North. The stockholders had already voted to replace the Negroes with white workers as soon as their contracts expired. In the meantime, he had the opportunity to observe them in action, and very shortly became convinced that "it would be decidedly for the interest of the Stockholders still to retain in their employ a large proportion of black hands." The stockholders agreed and even hired several slaves who had never before

[10] Cook, *The Life and Legacy of David Rogerson Williams,* 140; J. N. Williams to James Chesnut, March 12, 1835, in David R. Williams Papers.
[11] See also E. M. Lander, Jr., "Slave Labor in South Carolina Cotton Mills," *Journal of Negro History,* XXXVIII (April, 1953), 161–73.

been in a cotton mill. Graves professed that he had "never seen an equal number of entirely new hands become efficient operatives in less time." He found that the Negroes' imitative faculties were highly cultivated "so that whatever they see done they are very quick in learning to do." The Saluda carding and spinning rooms were operated by slaves almost entirely, he said, "and they perform their duties as promptly and as well as any hands I have ever seen."

A week later another correspondent wrote a letter in defense of the use of slaves in factories, but he approached the subject from a different viewpoint. To limit slave labor only to menial and agricultural pursuits would cause the Negroes in the course of time to become depressed and to become burdens on their masters. "For one, I must look upon any restrictions on African Slavery as manifesting *distrust in the institution and fatal to it in the end.*" [12]

Of those who opposed the use of slaves in cotton mills William Gregg was an outspoken leader. In 1845 he had favored the use of slaves because they did not have to be educated, and they were not able to move from one place to another as did the whites.[13] But later, in an address to the newly-created South Carolina Institute, he proposed that all labor in textile establishments be confined to white operators only. He stated that no mill had succeeded where Negro labor was permitted. Quite obviously Gregg's experience with white labor at Graniteville had encouraged his change of mind.

The Charleston *Mercury*, reporting Gregg's speech, took exception to the industrialist's remarks. The editor declared Gregg's argument false in theory and practice, and he noted that several factories in the state were operating successfully at the moment with slaves. One member of the institute, with obvious reference to the Free Soil Party of 1848—so hated in the South—denounced Gregg's opinions as identical with "*Free Soil and Free Labor.*" Solon Robinson, a Westerner traveling in the

12 *Daily Telegraph* (Columbia), May 7, 23, 30, 1849.
13 Gregg, *Domestic Industry*, 21.

South at that time, caustically observed that Gregg preferred
white workers because they were cheaper, and they were free
agents, "which also means they are free to starve if unable to
work; while the slave is always provided for at his master's expense." [14]

Both sides continued to argue the question for some time,
but years of experience had already proved that the Negro could
be a capable cotton mill operative, if properly trained and managed. Consequently, the decisive factor in determining his use
hinged upon the relative cost of slave and free labor. During the
1820's Hill and Clark, as previously shown, hired children for
$1.25 to $2.00 per week and weavers for $6.00 per week. For
over thirty years thereafter, no appreciable change occurred in
white workers' wages. Statistics from thirteen cotton mills in
1860, Graniteville excepted, reveal that they paid their female
employees an average of $89.04 each per year and their male
workers $138.96. It should be kept in mind that a considerable
number of children were included in each group.[15]

It is more difficult to determine the exact cost of Negro labor,
for in many instances the slaves were paid board in addition
to the wages their masters received. Too, the figures for several
plants are at considerable variance with each other. David R.

[14] Charleston *Mercury*, April 3, 1849; Herbert A. Kellar, ed., *Solon
Robinson, Pioneer and Agriculturist: Selected Writings* (2 vols.; Indianap-
olis, 1936), II, 212–14. A by-product of the controversy was the spread of
some alarm in the North. The New York *Herald* wrote: "Slave labor has
not yet been extensively introduced into the Southern manufactories, and
when that is introduced, it will demonstrate that the South can drive the
Eastern manufacturers out of their own markets in the manufacture of
coarse goods." Quoted in the *Daily Telegraph* (Columbia), August 11,
1849.

[15] Figures compiled by this writer from Eighth Census, Products of Industry, South Carolina (MS in South Carolina Department of Archives
and History). Several factories were not included because of obvious discrepancies in the returns. The wages of white overseers likewise showed
little variation between the 1820's and the 1850's. As seen, Colhoun hired a
superintendent for his small plant for $500 a year; Hill and Clark paid
William Bates $1.50 a day. In 1860 Vaucluse, a much larger firm, paid
only $2.25 a day for a general overseer. See Letterbooks, J. J. Gregg & Co.,
II, 323.

Williams estimated in 1828 that the labor of Negro children would cost only $25 each per year. On the other hand, in 1830 he hired three Negroes for $80 each per year. Seven years later at Vaucluse, George McDuffie asked $140 each for the use of five of his slaves for the ensuing year. Marlboro in 1849 hired five Negroes at an average annual rate of $96, and J. Graves in 1851 estimated that slave labor at Saluda cost an average of $75 per year. His figures included children.[16] But the cost of black labor, whatever it may have been, was influenced by two major factors over which the South Carolina textile manufacturer had no control: the price of cotton and the supply of slaves.

With the expansion of the cotton belt into the states of the Southwest, the demand for slaves soon outran the supply. Temporary setbacks notwithstanding, slave prices consequently rose steadily from 1820 to 1860. About 1850 the increasing cost of slave labor in South Carolina tipped the scales in favor of white workers. Vaucluse was reported to have stopped using Negroes. Marlboro had reduced its force of slaves to five. DeKalb was gradually replacing its slaves with white laborers because "they are less difficult to procure," and in 1853 completed the change-over. During the same year Saluda sold all of its Negroes. In fact Daniel McCullough at Mount Dearborn was the only cotton mill proprietor in South Carolina who continued to rely on slave labor. In 1860 his factory, employing a dozen hands and apparently operating only part time, used Negroes for all tasks but that of overseer.[17]

For the most part the mills experienced little difficulty in recruiting a sufficient number of white operatives from local sources. Their main problem was that of securing dependable workers. After a year's operations at Vaucluse, James Gregg was

[16] Williams to James Chesnut, October 26, 1828, May 14, 1830, in David R. Williams Papers; Martin, "The Advent of William Gregg," 402; *De Bow's Review*, VII (November, 1849), 458, XI (September, 1851), 319–20.
[17] Kellar, *Solon Robinson*, II, 218–19; Camden *Journal*, June 30, 1849; Camden *Weekly Journal*, January 18, August 2, 1853, Charleston *Daily Courier*, January 4, 1853; Eighth Census, Products of Industry, South Carolina: Chester District.

Table 3

Average Price of Prime Field Hands
(1805–1860)

Year	S.C.	New Orleans	Year	S.C.	New Orleans
1805	$550	$ 600	1835	$ 750	$1,150
1810	500	900	1837	1,200	1,300
1813	450	600	1844	500	700
1819	850	1,100	1846	650	750
1820	725	970	1851	750	1,150
1822	650	700	1852	800	1,200
1825	500	800	1853	900	1,250
1828	450	770	1855	900	1,350
1830	450	810	1858	950	1,580
1832	500	900	1859	1,100	1,690
			1860	1,200	1,800

Source: Alfred H. Conrad and John R. Meyer, *The Economics of Slavery, and Other Studies in Econometric History* (Chicago, 1964), 76, 84–91.

convinced that his employees "with but few exceptions" were so unreliable that he sent to New York for two large Irish families. Another annoyance was the constant shifting of some hands from one factory to another. Soon after Gregg reopened Vaucluse, James G. Gibbes at Columbia Mills sought to reach an agreement with him to prevent the irritating practice. At first Gregg was disinclined to impose such a restraint on his workers, but within a few months he had changed his views and agreed with Gibbes to allow no further movement between Vaucluse and Columbia Mills.[18]

An overseer at an Augusta mill during the period 1858–60 later declared that the Southern white workers were not willing

[18] Letterbooks, J. J. Gregg & Co., I, 135, II, 235, 246; *Daily Telegraph* (Columbia), March 10, 1849.

to subject themselves to a sufficient amount of discipline to operate a mill profitably. To do so, they felt, would be to place themselves on the same level with the Negro. Whether or not the average worker actually reasoned in that manner may be open to question. At any rate, the same overseer reported that absenteeism had been so prevalent, at least in Augusta, that in order to keep the machinery running "it became necessary to send out to the houses and drum in recruits." [19]

William Gregg recognized the difficulty involved in placing workers in a factory and then expecting them to knuckle under to distasteful regulations. And because he felt that cities fostered vice and evil, he looked upon city workers as most unreliable. He therefore advised the establishment of factories in rural areas. There, through a carefully planned policy of paternalism, the owners could indoctrinate their employees with the proper factory discipline.[20]

Gregg's system was common among the mill proprietors in the state. It consisted of furnishing the laborers not only with jobs but also with homes, churches, and schools, at the same time establishing rigid rules for the betterment of their morals. The workers thus became more and more dependent upon the owners, who were generally described by the local press as being benefactors of mankind. When Daniel McCullough built his factory on the Catawba, one laudatory editor declared that one of McCullough's objectives was "to give employment to and improve the moral condition of a class of people in that neighborhood who are living now in comparative wretchedness and vice." [21]

Graniteville, according to a Charleston newspaper, had benefited the indolent corrupted group of whites, who eked out a miserable existence in the sand hills. The schools did not reach them; the legislators corrupted them; they drank, quarreled, and

[19] M. F. Foster, "Southern Cotton Manufacturing," *Transactions* of the New England Cotton Manufacturers' Association, No. 68 (1900), 164–67.
[20] Gregg, "Practical Results of Southern Manufactures," 779–85.
[21] *Southern Chronicle* (Columbia), April 30, 1845.

fought. But at Graniteville they had been subjected to "Prussian discipline," which was wise, for it had bettered their condition and added wealth to the state. William Gregg's "philanthropy and patriotism" were responsible for their improvement. Gregg wrote: "We may regard ourselves [Graniteville] as the pioneers in developing the real character of the poor people of South Carolina." [22]

One of the first rules for the regulation of the worker's moral conduct was the prohibition of alcohol on the factory premises. The proprietors at Fingerville—Finger, Cannon, and Kestler— even agreed to keep no spiritous liquors in their private possession. McCullough unsuccessfully tried to secure a state law prohibiting alcohol in the vicinity of his establishment; and at Bivingsville, a visitor noted that Elias C. Leitner closed the factory in order that the workers might attend a temperance celebration. [23]

Graniteville was the most noted temperance stronghold of all the mill villages. Not only were prospective employees required to take the pledge before receiving jobs, but the purchasers of town lots from the company found total abstinence clauses inserted in the deeds to the property. Moreover, on occasion William Gregg enforced the clause. His fear of the evil influence of alcohol was shown, for instance, in a letter regarding one Morris, who, in violation of the law, sold whiskey near Graniteville: "He puts himself at defiance & has the most boisterous nuisance that has ever been within 5 miles of Graniteville. . . . Most of our reformed drunkards have returned to the bottle and lay about this nuisance day & night." Gregg predicted that if

[22] Gregg, "Practical Results of Southern Manufactures," 788–89; Charleston *Courier*, September 10, 1849. A Fourth of July toast to Dr. James Bivings by one of the workers, a close friend, praised him for being a "kind Father marching us onward to some higher calling." July 4, 1842, Diary of William Anderson (MS in possession of William D. Anderson, Gastonia, N.C.).

[23] Spartanburg Deeds, AA, 510–13; *Palmetto State Banner* (Columbia), December 18, 1849; *Spartan* (Spartanburg), March 27, 1851.

the place were not closed it would also ruin half the women and children of Graniteville in less than a year.[24]

The larger factories furnished homes for their workers and usually provided them with churches and schools also. The Graniteville Manufacturing Company helped finance the building of the Methodist and Baptist churches there. James H. Taylor reported that the Sabbath was regarded with reverence and the worship of God "strictly attended." On Sunday morning all the children, including Gregg's, met under one roof for Sunday school services, where the best educated and most respected of the workers acted as teachers. At DeKalb the proprietors had only one church; hence, their arrangement for Sunday school was similar to Graniteville's. In the evening they held preaching services with pastors of different denominations alternating from Sunday to Sunday. Even Fourth of July celebrations were tinged with religious ceremony. In 1853 the Graniteville workers first marched to church and listened to an oration from one of the ministers. The feast followed later.[25]

Graniteville and Vaucluse would hire no employees less than twelve years old, and all their workers' children between ages six and twelve were compelled to attend school. The Graniteville Academy, endowed with $10,000 by Ker Boyce in 1854, was a four-room school with three teachers. In 1860 its average daily attendance was about a hundred pupils. Gregg acted as his own truant officer and meted out swift punishment to any village urchin whom he caught playing hooky.[26] DeKalb, Crawfordsville, Bivingsville, and Fingerville are known to have had

[24] Gregg to S. W. Gardner, December 13, 1860, Letterbooks, J. J. Gregg & Co., II, 415. Gregg forced one Joseph Wooley to surrender title to a lot in Graniteville for having sold liquor. See Wallace, "Gregg and Graniteville," 49.

[25] Wallace, "Gregg and Graniteville," 46; J. H. Taylor, "Manufactures in South Carolina," *De Bow's Review*, VIII (January, 1850), 28; Charleston *Courier*, September 8, 1849; Charleston *Daily Courier*, July 9, 1853; Camden *Journal*, June 30, 1849.

[26] Letterbooks, J. J. Gregg & Co., I, 302; Charleston *Daily Courier*, January 27, 1860; Broadus Mitchell, *William Gregg, Factory Master*, 79–80.

schools, and it is likely that many of the other mill communities also possessed facilities for the education of the workers' children. The paternalistic policies of the factory owners, according to most accounts, were highly successful and beneficial to the workers. Gregg pictured Graniteville as an ideal community, as virtuous as any in the state. Seventy-nine of one hundred grown girls, upon first coming to Graniteville, he said, could neither read nor write, but "that reproach has long since been removed." Many of the workers had savings accounts; some had purchased pianos; others bought silk dresses. They enjoyed the luxuries of country life, yet teachers, lecturers, and musicians found patronage among them. Gregg told the stockholders that "our system has more than realized our expectations. We have always had a pressure upon us for situations, and could in a month stock another factory." [27]

A writer who visited DeKalb found the workers comfortably housed and their spiritual and temporal interests well cared for. He reported the following conversation with one of the girl employees:

Do you receive attention when you are sick?

A great deal more now than we used to; when we are sick, we have only to let the visitors of the female benevolent society know it, and we want for nothing. . . . [B]efore, though sometime we did get attention, yet there was a chance about it, which kept us uneasy. . . .
Some folks, continued she, look down upon factory folks, but I have had to work hard all my life, and I think a female better paid for work and less exposed here, than anywhere else she could get it. This is pretty constant, but it is not so hard as field work. I am thankful, to be as well off, as I am.[28]

The Vaucluse workers, so it was said, had been saved from poverty and crime and trained to sobriety and industry. For a

[27] Gregg, "Practical Results of Southern Manufactures," 788–89; Graniteville Stockholders' Minutes, June 22, 1859.
[28] Camden *Weekly Journal*, August 2, 1853.

woman there, as elsewhere, "one false step forever blasts her fame." However, only one expulsion had been necessary during the past seven years.[29]

Occasionally a discordant note was heard above the general tones of approbation. William Thomson, an Englishman who spent several days at Vaucluse in 1840, noted with dissatisfaction that the village was poorly located for getting the comforts and conveniences of life. "I did not consider the situation of the hands at all enviable." William Cullen Bryant, upon visiting a mill in the Augusta region, noticed that the girls for the most part had "a sallow, sickly complexion, and in many of their faces, I remarked that look of mingled distrust and dejection which often accompanies the condition of extreme, hopeless poverty." Before accepting Bryant's unfavorable comment at face value, however, one should consider his philosophy. As an abolitionist he possibly viewed the plight of workers under a paternalistic system as being not much better than slavery itself.[30]

One of the weakest points in the paternalistic system appeared to be that of the long work hours. Twelve or thirteen hours per day, six days a week, was the usual work-rule in South Carolina as elsewhere. One writer, under the pseudonym of "Pro Bono Publico," thoroughly castigated William Gregg on that score. He prefaced his remarks with the following statement: "Those articles which have appeared in the public papers from time to time, on the enterprising village of Graniteville, have always been one sided. They give but the sentiments of the stockholders, and are written by those who depend entirely on them for their information." He went on to say that he had conversed with several friends who had children in the factory and

[29] *Daily Telegraph* (Columbia), September 14, 1848. The workers at Vardry McBee's factory possessed a "neat appearance"; their homes were attractively and comfortably arranged with gardens of ample size, "the whole wearing a cheerful and happy appearance." *Keowee Courier* (Pickens), July 3, 1858.

[30] William Thomson, *A Tradesman's Travels, in the United States and Canada, in the Years 1840, 41 & 42* (Edinburgh, 1842), 113–14; William Cullen Bryant, *Letters of a Traveller; or Notes of Things Seen in Europe and America* (New York, 1850), 346–47.

therefore felt qualified to present the workers' viewpoint. The
"one great evil" of long hours, against which the people had
protested in vain, outweighed all the benefits the company offered. Many persons, he claimed, were awaiting an opportunity
to return to their original vocations.

"Pro Bono Publico's" criticism of Gregg was perhaps too
severe, but he was undoubtedly correct in representing the
opinion of some of the workers. When Gregg ran for the state
senate in 1858, his political opponents made capital of the issue
by publicly accusing him of being a cruel grinder of the poor in
the Graniteville factory.[31] How important a factor it was in his
defeat may only be conjectured.

---

[31] Edgefield *Advertiser*, November 21, 1850; Wallace, "Gregg and Graniteville," 127–29.

Chapter 7 Problems in Production & Marketing

While most factories exhibited a consistent and somewhat paternalistic attitude toward their workers, many showed more flexibility in their production policies. They shifted from one type of goods to another; albeit, the total result produced no marked change in the variety of yarns or woven goods offered. Whereas one plant might decide to concentrate on yarn and give up weaving, as did Vaucluse in 1859, another factory, Batesville for instance, installed looms and curtailed the sale of yarn. Generally, however, the products were coarse yarn, plain and striped osnaburgs, bleached and unbleached shirting and sheeting, and woolen cloth of several varieties for slaves' use. Other articles were likewise tried from time to time. McBee's factory, under John Hagarty's supervision in 1845, turned out some medium yarn, numbers 30 to 50. A few years later DeKalb advertised rope for plow lines, and in 1860 Vaucluse experimented with sewing thread.[1]

A product which at one time received considerable publicity and seemed to augur well as a lucrative source of income was cotton bagging, designed to take the place of hemp for baling purposes. Some earlier mills had tried it, but little was produced until 1841 or 1842, at which time Saluda and Society Hill began to manufacture it in large quantities. Saluda offered it for 20 cents a yard and claimed it to be more satisfactory than hemp. An interested promoter of bagging factories published information from Dr. James Bivings to show that for $10,000 an establishment could be built to manufacture the product at a total cost of 17.3 cents per yard.[2]

In the fall of 1842 Saluda reduced the price of its bagging to

[1] Charleston *Courier*, February 27, 1845; Camden *Journal*, January 2, 1850; Letterbooks, J. J. Gregg & Co., II, 433.

[2] *Farmers' Gazette and Cheraw Advertiser*, January 19, 1842. As early as 1830, Vaucluse made cotton bagging. Charleston *Courier*, July 9, 1830.

18 cents per yard and cited several Charleston factors who had
no objection to cotton bagging and found no difficulty selling
bales wrapped in it. At Society Hill, John N. Williams announced his intention to pack his entire 1843 cotton crop in
cotton bagging. But in spite of favorable editorials, cotton bagging evidently was not as satisfactory as hemp or jute—certainly
less durable—and the planters were not won over to its accept-
ance. The movement quickly subsided, although Williams kept
up its manufacture on a limited scale for several years.[3]

Wool manufacturing was never extensively carried on by
textile mills in South Carolina. John E. Colhoun and David R.
Williams were pioneer woolen producers on a small scale during the late 1820's and early 1830's, but apparently no other
factory attempted it until Vardry McBee, in the late forties, began to manufacture linsey-woolsey. His shipments supplied a
wide region in the back country, and in 1850 he planned to send
woolen goods to the Charleston market.[4] At Grindal Shoals, J.
Starke Sims began to turn out wool plaids in 1853. However, the
only factory in antebellum South Carolina that manufactured
wool on a large scale was Columbia Mills. James G. Gibbes and
Company installed about $20,000 worth of woolen machinery
in 1858 and soon began to process thirty thousand pounds of
wool per month into kerseys, jeans, and plains, selling them for
20 to 40 cents per yard.[5]

Most of the woolen cloth made in the state was woven by hand
looms at home, and this mainly in the upcountry. Yet, the wool
had to be carded before it was ready for the domestic weaver;
consequently, there was considerable demand for the textile
mills to install machinery for that purpose. The Fingerville, Biv-

[3] *South-Carolinian* (Columbia), October 13, 1842; Camden *Journal,*
September 2, 1842; Charleston *Courier,* September 22, 1842; Pendleton
Messenger, August 4, 1843; *De Bow's Review,* V (February, 1848), 190.

[4] Charleston *Courier,* September 9, 1850; *Southern Patriot* (Greenville),
March 14, 1851. John N. Williams wrote on February 11, 1832, that his
machinery was idle for lack of wool. Williams to James Chesnut, in
Williams-Chesnut-Manning Papers, South Caroliniana Library.

[5] *Carolina Spartan* (Spartanburg), July 21, 1859; Charleston *Daily
Courier,* December 21, 1859; *Southron* (Orangeburg), July 6, 1859.

ingsville, Pendleton, McBee, and Lester factories added wool cards to their establishments, either in the regular plants or in separate shops.

There were also wool carding shops in the state that were entirely unconnected with any other form of textile processing. One of the earliest was put up in 1818 at Centreville, Pendleton District, by James Chapman of Pennsylvania. By 1860 there were twelve or fifteen wool carding establishments, including those connected with cotton mills, but all were small affairs, with none having a capital of more than $2,000 or requiring more than three workers to tend the equipment. Their combined production probably did not exceed $30,000 in value.[6]

In the field of marketing the methods employed on the eve of the Civil War varied little from those of the 1820's and 1830's. The owners continued to depend mainly upon the commission merchants. The coming of the railroads, of course, permitted them to sell their goods over a wider area than had been possible previously, and more concerns shipped yarn to Northern markets than they did before 1840. Vaucluse, Graniteville, Saluda, Society Hill, and Marlboro mills were numbered among those which sent their goods north. Normally, the Piedmont trade was carried on by wagons over western districts of North Carolina, South Carolina, and Georgia, but during the 1850's the railroads penetrated this area, thus cutting in on the wagon trade. A small amount of upcountry yarn also began to reach New York.[7]

From its inception Graniteville, according to Gregg, was successful in its sales policy. Many of its stockholders were Charleston businessmen who enjoyed the good will of the local whole-

[6] *Carolina Spartan* (Spartanburg), May 3, 1860; Pendleton *Messenger*, August 26, 1818; Seventh and Eighth Censuses, Products of Industry, South Carolina. This writer found evidence of ten wool carding shops operating in the fifties not mentioned by the census.

[7] Letterbooks, J. J. Gregg & Co., II, *passim;* Graniteville Stockholders' Minutes; *Daily South Carolinian* (Columbia), April 12, 1856; *De Bow's Review,* V (February, 1848), 190, VII (November, 1849), 458; Charleston *Daily Courier,* April 5, 1858.

sale merchants. As soon as Graniteville goods first appeared, they were taken by Charleston jobbers and pushed to every point of the country reached by the Charleston trade. Soon they were in demand by merchants in the Southeast.

Howland and Taft, a wholesale firm in Charleston, had charge of Graniteville's "domestic sales," or those in the South. In 1851 they sold $137,000 worth of Graniteville goods, for which they charged 2 percent commission. Gregg's "foreign sales"—Northern—were handled by four agencies in as many cities. Their commissions varied from 2½ percent for cash sales to 5 percent on credit sales where they guaranteed collection. Slightly more than $56,000 worth of goods were sold through the Northern agents in 1851. In the late fifties Graniteville generally sold goods on four to eight months' credit for negotiable paper. In case it needed ready cash, the company would discount some of its trade acceptances. During the Panic of 1857 the treasurer discounted notes at the rate of 15 percent per annum, so great was their need for short-term paper.[8]

In 1860 Vaucluse had selling agents in New York, Baltimore, and Philadelphia. C. N. Averill of Charleston handled its local sales and supervised the shipping of its products which were consigned to the Northern agents. On the other hand, Saluda found its marketing of yarn in the North to be unprofitable, and when James G. Gibbes and Company bought the factory in 1855, they switched back to osnaburgs because of a steady home demand for that article.[9]

The railroads, which afforded the South Carolina textile manufacturers easy access to the more distant markets, also brought in supplies of cotton goods produced by their Northern competitors. As far as business was concerned, the local merchant was quite naturally interested in profits, and he was not inclined to

[8] Gregg, "Southern Patronage," 495; Wallace, "Gregg and Graniteville," 96; June 22, 1859, Graniteville Stockholders' Minutes.
[9] Letterbooks, J. J. Gregg & Co., II, *passim; Daily South Carolinian* (Columbia), April 12, 1856.

patronize home industry if Northern manufacturers could supply him with cheaper and more salable articles. On one occasion the Saluda factory was caught by a sudden drop in the market and was forced to sell a considerable quantity of yarn in New York at whatever price it would bring. At the same time, having speculated on cotton, the proprietors did not reduce the local price on current production. The Columbia merchants were indignant. One bluntly stated that he would not support home industries that would not, or could not, furnish the articles he desired as cheaply as he could get them elsewhere, saying, "I care not whether it be Boston, Manchester, Dundee or Calcutta." Several years later a local editor declared that the practice at Saluda had created such an opposition to the company on the part of the surrounding merchants that the company never recovered.[10]

In marked contrast to a view he had held earlier, in 1860 William Gregg went so far as to accuse local merchants of hiding Graniteville goods under the counter because they could not make as much profit on them as they could on Northern-made products. He doubted that Graniteville goods could be found on shelves of one out of every five stores in nearby Edgefield. Gregg critically contended that Southern merchants, in general, were directly averse to home manufactures.[11]

The quality of goods was also a factor in sales. Although the local manufacturers frequently maintained that Yankee goods were of poor quality, ofttimes they lost business because their own goods were of poor quality. The DeKalb mill frankly advertised in 1848, "Our Cotton Yarn having recently suffered in reputation, we have changed our arrangements, and are now manufacturing it of a quality that we can safely recommend to our customers. By special attention to this department of our business, we are determined fully to re-establish the lost char-

[10] *Daily South Carolinian* (Columbia), April 12, 1856; *Southern Chronicle* (Columbia), October 12, 19, 1842.
[11] Gregg, "Southern Patronage," 496–97.

acter of our Yarn, and hope that our friends will give it a fair trial." [12]

Other factories experienced similar difficulties. Vaucluse inadvertently sent some mixed yarn to its Philadelphia and Baltimore agents, both of whom sent back complaints. James Gregg thereupon asked them to make every allowance to the customers and advised them that he would do everything possible to prevent a recurrence. He firmly declared: "We have always at Graniteville borne the highest character for good work. And are determined to get the same reputation for this mill." [13]

Of noteworthy interest were the changes in the policies of production and marketing by J. J. Gregg and Company at Vaucluse during 1860 and early 1861. By midsummer, 1859, the company had introduced several hundred new spindles and removed the looms altogether. Vaucluse immediately began to produce a variety of yarn of numbers from 5 to 20 for the markets in Philadelphia, New York, and Baltimore, but James Gregg soon realized that he lacked a sufficient number of spinning frames to profitably manufacture more than two or three numbers at one time. In March of 1860 he asked Wyman, Byrd and Company if they could supply a steady demand for number 8 yarn in Baltimore as he preferred to concentrate on numbers 8 and 20 alone. Shortly afterwards he turned down a request from his New York agent for number 5 yarn.

Market fluctuations caused Gregg no end of worry in trying to decide what type of yarn to make and where to send it. In April the New York market was dull; in May the price of 12's and 14's declined in Baltimore; and in August he requested his Baltimore agent to ship his yarn on hand to Hay and McDevitt, the Philadelphia agency which, it appears, was his best seller.

[12] Camden *Journal*, August 16, 1848. On February 10, 1830, David R. Williams, comparing Northern mill products with his own, wrote, "I am satisfied, the manufacturer cannot make as stout, for anything *under 10 cents*. They may send a better sample, but the article will come out differently." Williams to James Chesnut, in David R. Williams Papers.

[13] Letterbooks, J. J. Gregg & Co., II, 179. McBee also had difficulty. See Charleston *Courier*, February 19, 1845.

On October 29, after a request from Hay and McDevitt for 22's, James Gregg replied that Vaucluse was not prepared to spin such fine yarn to advantage. The company had intended to gear the mill that fall to manufacture finer yarns, "but feel now that we should act with much caution as there is much political excitement. and it is the *Unanimous* voice that if Lincoln is elected there must be a dissolution of the Union and a Southern Confederacy."

The election almost threw the company into a panic. Gregg wrote a friend in New York: "You will confer a favor by making strict inquiry concerning the house of Stebbins Hoyt & Co. . . . We do not know who to trust. Our state will go out of the Union in a few days." A few days later he asked James Webb to collect gold for a draft of $5,000 on Hay and McDevitt and ship it by Adams Express to the Bank of Hamburg. The political agitation had stagnated trade, and money was exceedingly difficult to procure as banks would no longer purchase drafts on private parties.

To his Philadelphia agent James Gregg confided that when secession came their business would be "knocked into a cocked hat," unless Congress would repeal the duty on yarn. Failure to do so would place South Carolina on the same footing as foreign nations. He said that he had sold his looms for three dollars each but would gladly pay twenty dollars apiece to get them back. To replace them Gregg frantically sought to purchase fifty from the North. After failing to receive a satisfactory reply from any of three firms to whom he had written, Gregg, on December 13, asked Benjamin and Reynolds, of Stock Port, New York, if they could deliver them immediately. He advised that the Charleston harbor would probably be closed in a few days because of secession; therefore the looms would have to be shipped to Savannah, and that done before January 16, "otherwise some obstruction may take place in the co[a]sting trade."

Regardless of what his previous views may have been, after secession became an accomplished fact, James Gregg was a typical fire-eater. He wrote to James Webb on January 14: "Georgia will go out of the Union this week then our provisional Congress will meet and form a Southern Confederacy. not one state of us ever to Join a New England State. We are now prepared and burning for an army of Yankees to land on our shore where we hope with open arms to welcome them—with bloody hands to a hospitable grave."

A letter to Hay and McDevitt three days later revealed that Gregg expected a war and planned to profit thereby. He instructed the Philadelphia agents thusly: "Do not make anymore sales on our a/c except at *full prices* unless [further] advised. We feel confident that cotton will go up as high as 15¢ if a war comes which we are confidently expecting and preparing for. We would under the circumstances have held for some time before taking 22¢."

Yet, Gregg apparently did not permit his ardent Southern nationalism to chill his close relations with businessmen in the North. He continued to send yarn to his agents in Philadelphia and elsewhere, and in order to hasten the re-equipping of Vaucluse he spent the month of February, 1861, touring the manufacturing centers of the East. He succeeded in obtaining part of his machinery before the war broke. Shipments of new spindles arrived March 8 and April 3 from Alfred Jenks, near Philadelphia, and by April 1, twenty-four new looms had been installed.

The last Northern shipment of yarn recorded in Gregg's letterbook was dated March 13, just one month to the day before the fall of Fort Sumter. The following day he wrote L. P. Walker, the Confederate Secretary of War: "We are putting up a lot of superior drill looms, and in fifteen or twenty days, will be able to turn out a large quantity of tent cloth thirty inches wide at short notice—Soliciting an order from your department." [14]

At nearby Graniteville the elder Gregg likewise tried to prepare his factory for secession. In early 1860 he purchased some new machinery from England. He visited several machine works in the North that summer, and as late as March 12, 1861, he was

[14] Letterbooks, J. J. Gregg & Co., I, 128–29, II, 120–21, 130–31, 161, 305, 358, 365–76, 382–83, 392–94, 409, 414, 440, 445, 450–52, 465–96.

feverishly writing John C. Whitin to hasten the new cards, heating and sprinkler pipes, and other machinery. Some of his purchases never arrived.[15]

The question naturally arises why were not more textile mills established in antebellum South Carolina? William Gregg's outstanding leadership and personal success at Graniteville quickly became well known. The Graniteville Manufacturing Company began paying dividends in 1849. By 1855 the annual rate reached 10 percent. The company by-passed a payment in 1858 but in 1860 it paid 20 percent. Less noticed was the profitability of Batesville, which increased its capital value from $20,000 in 1850 to $50,000 in 1860. Its proprietors sold the company in 1862 to a group of Charleston entrepreneurs for $300,000, presumably in Confederate currency.[16] The Pendleton Manufacturing Company paid 6½ to 7 percent in the early fifties.[17]

Nevertheless, textile manufacturing, by and large, was not very profitable. Batesville was the only South Carolina textile mill, with over a thousand spindles, to increase its capital more than 50 percent from the time of its founding to the Civil War. And offsetting the success of the few companies were the dismal failures of the many. Vaucluse underwent at least four complete changes in ownership before J. J. Gregg and Company put it on a paying basis in the late fifties. Bivingsville was sold to a third group of stockholders in 1855 for less than one-third of the original investment. In the same year Saluda also passed into the hands of a third group of stockholders, at a loss of five-sixths of the original investment. The South Tyger factory in Spartanburg District underwent six reorganizations in twenty years. Marlboro and DeKalb were in financial difficulty at the time fire destroyed each. Other examples could be offered. Transfer of ownership, records show, was nearly always accompanied by a

[15] Wallace, "Gregg and Graniteville," 144.

[16] Ibid., 90, 118. The chief stockholders in the Charleston group were Frazer and Company, 470 shares, and James H. Taylor, 100 shares. Greenville Deeds, Z, 676, 685.

[17] Accounts of the Estate of Thomas M. Sloan, 1849–54, Anderson Wills, Roll No. 1201.

financial sacrifice on the part of the sellers. This was certainly indicative of meager profits.

As a matter of fact, the limited capital and the production and marketing policies of the South Carolina mills clearly revealed the semi-domestic nature of the South Carolina industry. Most companies lived from hand to mouth; they were financially insecure and economically insignificant. The Civil War brought them varying degrees of prosperity, and most survived in some fashion for several years afterward. In 1880 at least eleven of the prewar mills were still in operation. Among these were Graniteville, Vaucluse, and Bivingsville, now known as Glendale after having undergone significant expansion.

Thus, the great cotton mill crusade begun in the 1880's saw the establishment of almost three million spindles in South Carolina within twenty-five years.[18] As this boom got under way, the small antebellum mills were forced either to modernize or to close. Even those which survived underwent changes in ownership and often in name. The Graniteville Manufacturing Company, owners of both Graniteville and Vaucluse, continued into the mid-twentieth Century under its original name, as did the Pendleton Manufacturing Company. Elsewhere cotton manufacturing has been maintained almost continuously on the approximate locations of the Bivingsville Manufacturing Company (Glendale), Hudson Berry's (Fork Shoals), Philip Lester's (Pelham), Fingerville, and Valley Falls. However, with the exception of the original Graniteville plant, all antebellum cotton factory buildings have long since been destroyed.

Outstanding among the antebellum entrepreneurs who played important roles in the postwar era were Dexter C. Converse and Henry P. Hammett. Converse, a native New Yorker, joined in the reorganization of Bivingsville in 1855. After the war he organized his own D. E. Converse Company, which later absorbed Bivingsville and other cotton mill properties. With part of his

---

[18]For data on post-1865 South Carolina textiles see Kohn, *The Cotton Mills of South Carolina* and Mitchell, *The Rise of Cotton Mills in the South.*

textile fortune he founded Converse College in Spartanburg. Hammett, son-in-law of textile pioneer William Bates, joined the Batesville partners in 1849 as business manager. In 1876 he established a modern textile factory of 10,000 spindles at Piedmont. Its immediate success gave encouragement to further expansion in the next decade.

Not to be overlooked was William Gregg. Although he died in 1867, Gregg's success at Graniteville and his many enlightening pamphlets and speeches in behalf of Southern textile manufacturing continued to be influential long after his death. He had stated in 1855 that the chief causes of failure among Southern cotton mills included injudicious selection of machinery; lack of steady, efficient, and cheap motive power; improper location of factories in cities instead of rural areas; neglect of the religious and moral training of the workers; and insufficient capitalization. He pointed to the failures of Saluda and Vaucluse as prime examples of the causes he named. To these five Gregg later added a sixth major factor, which was lack of Southern patronage.[19] He also might have mentioned another, and that was fire. The Fulton, Downs and White, Laurel Falls, DeKalb, and Marlboro factories all burned, never to rise again. The Hills and Weavers both suffered two fires each during their early history, and when Lester and Kilgore's factory burned in 1853, the local newspaper stated that it was the third time a cotton mill had been destroyed on that site. In the South the insurance rates on cotton factories were so high, said James E. Henry, that the manufacturers had to assume the risk themselves.[20]

The first two of Gregg's conclusions were largely supported by contemporary evidence. The third and fourth were probably negligible factors in determining profits. As for the fifth reason, it is true that too many firms tried to operate with insufficient

[19]Gregg, "Practical Results of Southern Manufactures," 779-86; William Gregg, "Southern Patronage," 229-30.
[20]Laurensville *Herald*, July 22, 1853. Henry placed the rate at 5 percent, but in 1860 James Gregg paid 1½ percent on Vaucluse, a granite factory building. *Speech of Maj. James Edward Henry, on Productive Corporations*, 14-15; Letterbooks, J. J. Gregg & Co., I, 175-81, II, 216.

capital. Yet, according to an analysis by Professor Alfred G. Smith, Jr., there appeared to be a "substantial supply of liquid capital available for investment" in South Carolina, especially among the Charleston entrepreneurs.[21] Whatever their relative merit, the five causes listed by Gregg in 1855 resulted from faulty planning or poor management. The lack of Southern patronage of which he complained in 1860 was due mainly to Northern competition, which had become increasingly keen after 1850.

During the fifties the whole textile industry in New England was involved in a cut-throat competition, and dividends of the leading cotton manufacturing companies dropped from a high of over 17 percent in 1845, to an average of 5.3 percent from 1848 through 1859. One of the largest firms, the Boston Manufacturing Company, averaged 9 cents per yard profit, 1820–25, but by 1850 it was fortunate to make over one-half cent profit per yard. On this basis, only large sales could bring profits sufficient enough for companies to remain in business. As a result, many of the small mills in New England were driven to the wall.[22]

Of the oftspoken advantages that South Carolina possessed relative to cheap power, cheap labor, and the proximity of raw materials, only one—cheap labor—proved to be of real benefit. During the early 1850's the labor cost per yard of cloth made at Graniteville hovered between 1.3 and 1.4 cents, while the Boston Manufacturing Company's labor cost varied from 2 to 2.5 cents per yard.[23] This difference alone was sufficient to permit the small South Carolina mills to remain in business so long as they

[21] Alfred G. Smith, Jr., *Economic Readjustment of an Old Cotton State*, 122–24.

[22] Ware, *New England Cotton Manufacture*, 85–86, 110, 152–54. If Graniteville had sold its entire cloth output in 1859 at a profit of only one-half cent per yard, the company would have netted only 5 percent on its capital investment. Eighth Census, Products of Industry, South Carolina: Edgefield District.

[23] Ware, *New England Cotton Manufacture*, 114. Graniteville labor costs for one week in 1853 are included in Wallace, "Gregg and Graniteville," 91.

were efficiently operated. South Carolina's, and the South's, dilemma was that the region had waited too long to give serious attention to industry. Meanwhile, textiles became firmly implanted in the North. By 1850 the South's competition from the North was similar to what New England faced vis-a-vis England in 1815. But whereas New England secured tariff protection, beginning in 1816, against her well-established competitor, the South could not avail itself of a similar remedy against the North. It is small wonder, therefore, that most Southern entrepreneurs, after a brief flurry of activity in the forties, were reluctant to pour further capital into textiles in the 1850's.

Yet, with the move for secession gaining momentum in South Carolina, it is to be wondered why the radicals did not encourage industry. William Gregg had warned as early as 1844 that agitators who wished to resist Congress or dissolve the Union should be anxious to diversify and render South Carolina economically independent of other countries. His advice went largely unheeded, for in the fifties, as in the thirties, the biggest hotheads were all too often the weakest proponents of industry. Their hatred of the North obviously blinded them to economic reality as they closed ranks around slavery and cotton culture. In the end Gregg and the state's business leaders, many of them Unionists at heart, surrendered to the hysteria that reigned in Charleston on December 20, 1860 [24] when, by unanimous vote, a convention specially called by the state legislature passed an ordinance dissolving "the union now subsisting between South Carolina and other States."

[24] See Lillian A. Kibler, "Unionist Sentiment in South Carolina in 1860," *Journal of Southern History,* IV (August, 1938), 346–66.

Index

Adams: Vardry McBee's overseer, 84

Allston, Governor R. F. W., 32n

Ancrum, Thomas J.: stockholder in DeKalb factory, 72

Anderson, William: organizer of the DeKalb factory, 42, 66, 72. *See* DeKalb factory

Arnold, Shubal F.: establishes cotton mill on Reedy River, 18–19

Ashley Manufacturing Company, 63

Averill, C. N.: Vaucluse agent in Charleston, 102

"A Voice From Graniteville," 61

Bank of Hamburg (S.C.), 105

Bates, William: buys Weaver's factory, 19–20; early textile career of, 20–21; overseer for Hill and Clark, 27; mentioned, 13n, 26, 77, 81n, 83, 90n, 109. *See* Batesville

Batesville: origin of, 21; increase of capital, 77; production policy of, 99; size of factory, 107; mentioned, 83, 109. *See* Bates, William

Bauskett, John: buys Vaucluse factory, 37–38; reports on Vaucluse, 45; opposes Graniteville charter, 56; mentioned, 48, 74. *See* Vaucluse Manufacturing Company

Beard's Falls, 38

Belvidere Manufacturing Company, 63

Benjamin and Reynolds, 105

Bennett, Governor Thomas, 32n

Bennett, Thomas, Jr.: investor in South Carolina Homespun Company, 7n

Bennettsville, 42

Benson, Enoch B.: partner in establishment of the Pendleton Manufacturing Company, 23

Berry, Hudson: acquires Arnold's factory, 18–19; mentioned, 78n, 108

Bivings, A. W., 73

Bivings, Dr. James: operates Lincolnton, N.C., cotton mill, 20, 21; establishes Bivingsville factory, 21–22; establishes mill on Chinquepin Creek, 66; establishes mill at Crawfordsville, 66–67; a "kind Father," 94n; mentioned, 26n, 71, 73, 83, 99. *See* Bivingsville Cotton Manufacturing Company

Bivings, James D.: son of Dr. James Bivings, 66, 78

Bivingsville Cotton Manufacturing Company: establishment of, 21–22; installation of looms, 25; number of employees, 26; capitalization of, 28; reorganization of, 73–74; supports school, 95; production polices of, 100–101; sale of, 107; absorbed by D. E. Converse Company, 108; mentioned, 51n, 77, 81n, 94

Blackwood, J. J.: leading investor at Graniteville, 78

Blanding, Shubal: director of Saluda Manufacturing Company, 38

Bobo, Simpson: investor in Hill's factory, 15; investor in Cedar Hill factory, 18; stockholder in Bivingsville, 21, 73; mentioned, 16, 22, 26n

122

INDEX

Walker and Saunders: construction
engineers, 64
Wallace, Peter M.: buys or leases
South Tyger factory, 77
Waring, Benjamin: Stateburg in-
vestor, 5
War of 1812: effect on South Caro-
lina manufacturing, 10
Watson, Tillman, 86
Weaver, Francis A.: partner in Ce-
dar Hill factory, 18; partner of
William Bates, 20
Weaver, John: partner in South
Carolina Cotton Manufactory,
14; establishes mill in Greenville
District, 14, 19; establishes mill
at Valley Falls, 71; mentioned,
13n, 14n, 18, 20, 26n, 27
Weaver, Lindsey: textile entrepre-
neur from Rhode Island, 13
Weaver, Philip: textile entrepre-
neur from Rhode Island, 13; agent
for the Weavers, 14; leaves the
South, 14
Weaver, Wilbur: textile entrepre-
neur from Rhode Island, 13
Weavers The: partnership of John,
Philip, and Lindsey Weaver, and
others, 16, 20, 25, 26, 109
Webb, James, 105
Wells, Thomas: director of Saluda
Manufacturing Company, 38
Welsman, James T.: director of
Charleston Cotton Manufactur-
ing Company, 63
White, Robert: partner in Laurens
District cotton mill, 25
White, William: partner in Lau-
rens District cotton mill, 25
Whitin, John C.: Northern ma-
chinery manufacturer, 107
William Anderson and Company,

42. See Anderson, William
William Mason and Company,
Taunton, Mass.: sells spindles to
Gregg, 60
Williams, Governor David R.: or-
ganizes Society Hill factory, 10-
11; reorganizes Society Hill factory, 32-35; death of, 34; labor
force and labor policies of, 11,
42-44; production policies of, 44,
100; Northern competition of,
47-48; cost of slave labor, 90-91;
mentioned 13, 32n, 45, 88, 104n
Williams, John N.: inherits David
R. Williams share in Society Hill
factory, 34; partner in Marlboro
factory, 41, 71; produces cotton
bagging, 100; mentioned, 42, 88,
100n
Willson, Hugh: partner with Bates
in mill in Larens District, 20
Willson, Vincent: father of two
child-employees of Hill and
Clark, 26
Wilkinson, James G. O.: president
of Vaucluse Manufacturing Company, 37
Wofford, Benjamin: financial
backer of South Carolina Cotton
Manufactory, 14; investor in Cedar Hill factory, 18
Wofford's Iron Works, 21
Wooley, Joseph: Gregg forces him
to surrender lot, 95n
Wyman, Byrd and Company, 104

Yeadon, Richard, 32n
Young, A.: stockholder in DeKalb
factory, 72

Zimmerman, John C.: member of
John Bomar and Company, 73-74

DATE DUE

DEC 1 8 1984			
GAYLORD			PRINTED IN U.S.A.